Inspiring Entrepreneur Stories

10 Success Stories From the World of Business and Lessons to Help You Succeed

Lars De Veer

from various sources. Please consult a licensed professional before attempting any techniques outlined in this book.

By reading this document, the reader agrees that under no circumstances is the author responsible for any losses, direct or indirect, that are incurred as a result of the use of the information contained within this document, including, but not limited to, errors, omissions, or inaccuracies.

Table of Contents

Introduction

Success, especially in business, can often seem elusive. When you begin your journey to make a name for yourself as an entrepreneur, you will learn, and quickly too, that a good idea is not enough. Your execution of those ideas will determine whether you will become a serious competitor in your industry or close up shop.

This book, ***Inspiring Entrepreneur Stories***, details the journey of triumphant entrepreneurs. You, the reader, will learn how to properly execute your ideas from the choices of these exemplary businesspeople.

And in today's sea of flashy new businesses, allow this diverse set of success stories to fill you with hope that you too can stand out and live your dreams.

Chapter 1:

Finance

The financial industry is riddled with more success stories than we can count. Each year, we see a new breakthrough disrupting the industry, pushing us to conquer newer ways of handling, making, saving, and growing money. But this story isn't about all the big names that stole the limelight. It's about a little boy's dream to make his family some money.

Enter Afterpay.

Since its inception, Afterpay has been a global sensation due to its growth and strides in the market in its short period of existence. For decades, layaways have been the order of the day when consumers are unable to meet the price tags of items. Without a better system, consumers faced exorbitant interest rates and inane policies that were often cringey to think about on a normal day. But all that came to change when a young entrepreneur from Australia applied a millennial twist to buying things on credit and created a better system that spiraled into a multinational business. Thus began Afterpay, a consumer-lending organization formed in Sydney, Australia. The business has since attained a market value of over $1.5 billion in less than four years since its inception.

Nick Molnar, co-founder and CEO whose idea formed the brain of the system, has attained a net worth of about $200 million. The business was easily successful in his native country of Australia—a feat he is trying to replicate in the United States and other regions across the globe. Afterpay first started operating during the early period of 2015 and got listed on the Australian Exchange (ASX) through an IPO raising $25 million sometime in mid-2016, trading at a share price of $1. However, in recent times, the company's shares sell for more than $70, which is over 190% return per year across the past years since its inception. Participants in the IPO who stayed by the business through thick and thin have doubtlessly had their faith repaid big time.

Nick Molnar was raised in Sydney, where he began an online store on eBay while in college. He sold jewelry as a part of the family business and was so good at sales and marketing that he rose to the rank of top jewelry seller in the entire Australian eBay. In a bid to take on more challenges, Molnar reached out to Ice.com, a jewelry site based in the United States, convincing them to let him launch an Australian outpost . To say Molnar was successful would be an understatement, because he grew the business to rake in $2 million in yearly revenue. During the time of his growth, Molnar had a neighbor, Anthony Eisen, who was the then chief investment officer at Australian holding company Guinness Peat Group. Molnar was usually up all night doing his business, as was Eisen, who couldn't help but notice the other night owl across the road from his place. One morning, Eisen found Molnar and introduced himself.

From then on, the two got along pretty well. Eisen, being the savvy corporate executive, lent Molnar a helping hand with some mentorship and introduced the young entrepreneur to several people in his business network. By 2015, Molnar had created one of the largest local distribution chains for jewelry online. Life couldn't be better! But young Molnar was very much unsatisfied, frustrated even. The business was starting to experience low conversion rates of visitors on the site. The problem began to grow, giving Molnar the option of keeping his position as top dog or falling down the pecking order. There was only so much time before the competition caught up to him. He pondered improving sales through large and recurring orders, and came up with a system. Molnar rolled out the first system of Afterpay, which revolved around a simple instalment plan option for payment. After integrating it into the website, he noted a significant improvement in the metrics that were the main drivers of the business.

The plan was simple. Molnar discovered that consumers considered breaking down a $100 item into quarterly instalments of $25 as a more attractive alternative to a one-off payment at checkout. Thus began the system of Afterpay, which followed soon afterwards as a full-blown organization in mid-2015. The two founders had complementary skills: Eisen had the experience and street savviness of an elite corporate executive and Molnar was a young, talented entrepreneur with all the doggedness and experience needed to thrive. Couple that with a great support team made up of the finest individuals in their respective fields, such as David Hancock (finance), Fabio De Carvalho (sales), Craig Baker (technical lead), Barry Odes (COO), and David Whiteman (product), and the business was impeccably angled for greater growth in the long run.

Molnar's theory for running the business was simple. He believed millennials expressed a strong aversion for credit cards because they almost always led to compounding debt. So, Afterpay was born in a bid to allow consumers to pay for purchases in quarterly instalments devoid of interest. With this system, a shopper can procure an item of $100 and make an upfront payment of $25, and $25 payments subsequently every two weeks until the initial cost is covered. If the consumer misses a payment, they will have to pay an initial late fee of $8, after which they will be charged $8 weekly if no further payments are made. However, the late fees cap at 25% of the total value of the item, as a hedge against unforeseen contingencies.

Afterpay gets the bulk of its revenue from a different source. The business charges retailers 4-6% of every transaction to use the service. With Afterpay, consumers can purchase goods up to $1,000. Following the launch of the organization in October 2014, about two years later, Molnar happened on a stroke of genius. The business was starting to gain traction, so he took a gamble and encouraged clients to get in touch with their favorite retailers and ask that they use Afterpay services. Needless to say, that was a huge success. The campaign went viral on social media and the company soared. Afterpay had struck a nerve with young shoppers due to Molnar's theory of being credit aversive. In a 2016 survey by Bankrate.com, one in three adults between the ages of 18 to 29 owned a credit card.

According to Matt Harris, managing director at Bain Capital Ventures and popular fintech investor, "The financial crisis scarred a generation into not doing stupid things with their finances. They're kind of scared with credit." In Australia in recent times, the average age of consumers that use Afterpay is around 33 years. Also, eight in 10 of them are women. Many retailers jumped onto the service because as soon as they partnered with Afterpay, they saw a significant increase in customer orders from 20-50%. Some retailers even had more success, as up to one quarter of their online orders were processed via the pay-later services shortly after joining the Afterpay service. Since then, Afterpay has grown to offer its services to more than over two million customers and 15,000 retail partners.

According to Molnar, the company manages credit checks by considering several hundred data points, while the underwriting model focuses on the products. For instance, if there is a strong demand among consumers for a specific luxury item, such as a high-end dress, Afterpay is more likely to reject such a transaction. The reason for this rejection stems from the fear that fraudsters may turn around, flip the purchase for cash at a much reduced price, and bail out on their next couple of Afterpay payments. The business also analyzes the Afterpay payment history of a consumer to determine their creditworthiness. On a large scale, Afterpay rejects up to 20% of their usual transactions for the above reason. In one year, the company had to write off under 1% of their entire sales because consumers could not pay their loans.

Afterpay went public under Molnar in 2016, after managing to raise $25 million. He commented on the capital industry in Australia, saying there was no venture capital market. Afterpay processed up to $561 million in its 2017 fiscal year, which resulted in $23 million in revenue and about $10 million in net loss. As of 2019, Afterpay was on track to rake in $80 million in revenue by processing $2 billion in sales. With the company trading at a valuation of $1.5 billion, the projected valuation of investors sits at a whopping 19 times sales. This is a mind-blowing valuation, which is more than 10 times as much as other new lenders on the block like Lending Club and OnDeck. Since 2017, the sales growth of Afterpay in Australia alone has leveled off. The business got around 3,000 to 5,000 new customers daily in 2019, which was the same number as the year before that. According to Molnar, the numbers were a result of Afterpay already bringing on the largest retailers in the region.

As of 2019, Molnar was trying to quicken the growth of the business by introducing it to the United States. Not long after, Urban Outfitters made a public announcement about offering Afterpay services. However, the plan for continued expansions in the future may be seemingly more difficult than it was years back when the business first began. Affirm, an outfit in San Francisco dating back to 2012, was created by the founder of PayPal, Max Levchin. The company offers consumers low-interest loans and has clients in the single-digit millions. Seeing Afterpay's move to the U.S. market, Elizabeth Allin, a spokesperson for Affirm, was of the opinion that Afterpay was hoping for lightning to strike twice in the United States following its great growth in Australia. According to Allin, "We know how long it takes to grow and sustain a consumer brand."

Klarna, a Stockholm-based outfit, is another consumer finance provider created in 2005. The business raked in up to $524 million in revenue in 2018 alone. Klarna's influence in the European region is strong, but its progress has reportedly dragged in the United States and the United Kingdom. According to a Klarna spokesperson, the company is taking a long-term view, which is a critical position in a market like the United States. The spokesperson went on to add that, "Markets are very different landscapes and we take the time to understand consumer behavior, merchant needs, identify what we are trying to solve and then we adapt our product accordingly."

With competitors flunking in the competitive landscape that is the U.S. market, Afterpay seems to have its work cut out for it. But Molnar thinks differently. He feels that consumers would view the business differently from other competitors as there are no interests or charges levied on their purchases. Besides, it's unlikely that anyone would be willing to take out a loan just to afford a pair of Jordans. And among millennials, who are only willing to spend the money they already have, Molnar believes in a shift in how people spend their money. And to him, that's all Afterpay focuses on solving.

In summary, Eisen and Molnar created an excellent company culture that prioritized focus, agility, and humility. What's more, both founders have taken turns being the CEO of the outfit, with Molnar originally taking the position before relinquishing it to Eisen as soon as the company got to a specific level. This goes to show the absence of ego between them, as well as the good working relationship they share—which can be considered as an ideal dynamic in the world of finance. The business has also been open to the ideas of its consumer base, investors, and merchants, and has been sensitive and well-informed about the necessity of regulatory changes in its novel industry. What's more, the company has a sole focus, which is demonstrated by the single product status they express. Also, Afterpay seems to have trumped the temptation to monetize its consumer base by focusing on key value drivers in the long term.

There are only a few companies that managed to capture the imagination of Australia like Afterpay. Not only did the business not exist eight years ago, but it's worth more than $7 billion now. What's more, its story is a good old cliche: a young founder pairs up with an older, more experienced professional while working tirelessly in his bedroom, grows the business to an exciting phenomenon within the country, takes on the rest of the world, is caught in the crosshairs of regulations and auditing, and ends up as a global sensation. To understand just how big a deal the company has become since its inception, consider the following: the two biggest and most successful e-commerce businesses in Australia are Catch of the Day and Logan. These businesses are worth $230 million and $441 million respectively, and have been active for more than a decade before Molnar came into the scene with Afterpay. Then there's one of the biggest fintechs to come out of Australia, Props, which is worth around $565 million. Even Australia's most successful retailer in the last two decades, JB Hi-Fi, has a net worth in the region of $3 billion—which, as big as it sounds, isn't up to half of Afterpay's market value now.

The first quirk of fate for young Molnar was meeting Anthony Eisen, who was an ex-exec of Guinness Peat and Caliburn. The latter only noticed Molnar because they were both night owls, and that was enough to start a friendship. In time, Nick would come to share his ideas about Afterpay and what the system would be like. Basically, he proposed to use debit cards as some kind of virtual credit card by allowing payments in instalments over a 60-day period. Molnar's revelation was insightful to Eisen because many millennials, especially the younger ones, didn't own or care for credit cards. Also, Molnar's idea could sidestep the necessity of checks and approvals as it wasn't and still isn't considered a credit product. The system Molnar and Eisen had imagined turned out to be a good idea, but was hardly novel because Klarna, the Swedish-based outfit, was already a $3 billion organization at the time. Eisen was given the role of executive chairman, but worked as a CEO. Molnar assumed the title of CEO, even though he effectively worked as the head of sales, which was by far the key driving role in the success of Afterpay.

In the early stages, the duo didn't have a tech platform or a system that facilitated transactions and created a firewall algorithm that prevented fraud. This would be the first of Afterpay's problems, but they soon found a way around it. To solve the looming security problem, Molnar and Eisen found a Melbourne-based business listed on the ASX. The organization known as Touch Payments was created in 2000 and had listed on the Australian Exchange in 2015, having a valuation of over $160 million. Touch Payments seemed like a strong performer on the ASX. In 2016, Eisen and Molnar were able to list Afterpay on the Australian Exchange through a $25 million deal. However, that was not the end to their problems. Afterpay soon became heavily dependent on Touch Payments to create its technology, which led the latter to own a significant stake in Afterpay. Eventually, it came down to the fact that Afterpay was merely a huge bet on the ability of Molnar to develop and manage enterprise relationships.

In the latter periods of 2016, November precisely, tragedy struck with the death of Touch Payments' founder and CEO, Adrian Cleeve. The death of Cleeve was a huge blow for his company, leading to its share price taking a nosedive. All of a sudden, Afterpay, which was still a growing business, wasn't a dependent member of a partnership anymore. In 2017, Touch merged with Afterpay, with shareholders of the former owning around 35% of both enterprises. This deal helped to solidify the future of Afterpay, as Eisen and Molnar had acquired control of a valuable tech platform at little to no cost. Around the early periods of the merger, Molnar and Eisen appointed David Hancock, a non-executive director and one of their early investors, as a group head. In other words, Hancock was to play the role of acting CEO. On one hand, it seemed like a totally risky move—totally unnecessary and somewhat strange too, considering Eisen was still on the executive chair. Initially, Hancock's role involved overseeing the integration of both companies: Afterpay and Touch.

In a strange turn of events, many different articles started to paint Hancock as one of the co-founders of Afterpay. It was enough hard work deciphering if it was just lazy journalism, or if the newly appointed head implied as much in one of his interviews. The former seems more likely, because Hancock's role in the creation of Afterpay is as significant as a doorknob at an orchestra. By the time Hancock arrived to assume his role in the company, Afterpay had amassed 840,000 customers and 6,000 merchants. As far as the business goes, it's a market darling, especially among millennials, although a controversial one. Although Afterpay survived and navigated a Senate inquiry, which could well have resulted in coverage by the National Credit Act, it soon became entangled in an ill-timed Austrac audit. The regulator did not fail to announce its concerns regarding the compliance of the outfit with anti-money laundering laws.

With a vast market to be addressed, especially in Europe and the United States, Afterpay shows all the signs of being another global success story from the shores of Australia, just like Atlassian. Whatever the case, there's more to come from the company, and more literature to write on the Afterpay story.

Things You May Not Know About Nick Molnar

1. The highest degree achieved by Nick Molnar is a Bachelor's (BSc Commerce) from the University of Sydney.
2. Nick Molnar has held three positions in Afterpay since its creation:
    a. Chief Revenue Officer/Executive Director/CEO: United States/Co-Founder (07/2019–11/2020).
    b. Chief Revenue Officer & Executive Director (07/2019–Present).
    c. Co-CEO/Managing Director/Co-Founder (11/2020–Present)
3. During the early stages of Molnar's career, he worked as an Investment Analyst at venture

capital firm M.H. Carnegie & Co. While there, Nick's primary responsibility was growth-stage investments.

4. In April 2012, Molnar's first business, BeShop, joined the incubator program at M.H. Carnegie & Co..

5. Under Eisen's influence, Molnar interned at the Guinness Peat Group between February and March 2011. Prior to that, young Molnar interned at Investec Bank Australia for a month in 2009.

6. In January 2020, Nick Molnar won an award for Best Payment Innovation.

Things to Know as a Startup in the Financial Industry

1. Surround yourself with good advisors with the right industry experience peculiar to your business type. It's best if they also live within your location. With advisors, you will be able to leap and bound above some early mistakes that could prove inhibitive big time. Also, they could help you with connections to other advisors in the long run.

2. Don't hold back on selling your products. Get them out there as quickly as the business starts to grow. Not only will it help you validate yourself, but you'll also get constructive criticisms from paying clients.

3. Hire good people in your ranks, who are in alignment with the business and company culture. It's best you find and hire such people during the early periods of the business, as they are the one who will create and promote the company culture.

4. Never underestimate marketing and sales. From the beginning, ensure to be decisive about selling and marketing your product the right way to improve your chances of success.

Chapter 2:

Fintech

One of the most difficult things about creating a startup is that huge expectations fall on your shoulders. You are expected to be a pro at everything. Bootstrapping founders are quickly introduced to the reality of being the CEO, tech support, bookkeeper, janitor, customer service, and HR department all at once. And although it's not the worst job in the world to assume all these roles by yourself, you'll quickly realize that you have limitations and will have to call in the experts. One expert we'll be focusing on in this segment is Jessica Mah and her team of over 209 employees at the entrepreneur-centric accounting outfit, inDinero.

According to inDinero, the back office of any company can be seen as the administrative unit linked with the running of the business, including taxes and accounting. Or, "All of the boring stuff smart companies outsource to inDinero's accounting nerds!" Jessica Mah makes accounting look like the easiest thing to do. She first started inDinero while in middle school before going on to complete high school by age 15. Next, she went to UC Berkeley, where she studied computer science before founding InDinero in her dorm room. The outfit began as a platform for small-scale businesses to manage their finances before Mah got a spot at the prestigious Silicon Valley incubator YCombinator. She won up to $1.2 million in funding, which allowed her to grow InDinero to a platform that managed more than $2 billion in consumer transactions with a team of seven people.

Mah managed all of these feats before she reached the legal drinking age. But even as far as her feats go, she remains one of the most cool, collected, honest, and down-to-earth entrepreneurs in the industry. According to Mah, the idea for InDinero did not strike overnight. It was a lifelong battle she had to deal with over the years. Every other time she started a business (she had several before InDinero), she was in charge of building the products and had to do her own marketing. In the end, she was terrible with managing her finances—a bad habit she couldn't quite shake off. So one day, it occurred to her that she could get better at accounting, as she discovered it was a problem that didn't plague her alone but other startups as well. With a few more inquiries, she found out just how big a need it was— financial management for small-scale businesses. That was when it dawned on Mah that she could do something. So, pairing up with her co-founder Andy Su, the duo decided to start InDinero.

At the time, they were juniors at Berkeley. When they finished homework slightly earlier one fateful week, the duo decided to start a business for fun just to see where it led. That moment of playful insight was the starting point of InDinero. As school rolled by and the founders graduated, there came a point where they had to decide on whether or not to pursue their creation full-time. Their friends were applying for jobs, and Mah and Su discovered that they weren't really the nine to five types. So, they couldn't get themselves to apply for jobs like their mates, choosing instead to pursue their hobby. In retrospect, Mah believes she and Su would have found a normal workplace unbearable. It wouldn't help that they would turn out as terrible employees and end up getting the boot. So, more out of necessity than intent, they applied to YCombinator. It was imperative that their decision worked, or they just might be ruined. Suffice it to say, the startup chose them.

Mah reckoned that having a real job as an employee might have helped their cause a bit. It was their first job post-college, after all. This begs the question of whether or not their ages influence business in any way. Since they were quite the young founders, investors and customers could see the business in differing lights, but it was nothing Su and Mah couldn't handle. Customers didn't see it as a big deal, and Mah posits that younger business owners felt like they could relate because they were otherwise used to old, cranky accountants. It only made sense that they'd like Su and Mah better. As far as investors went, they didn't really care for the ages of the founders. Mah insists that being inexperienced and young wasn't the best of experiences. It was one thing to be young, but being experienced is an understated necessity.

The biggest challenges inDinero has faced since coming to the limelight bordered on company culture. Trying to stay grounded and humble was a struggle during the first year of the business.

You can try putting yourself in their shoes. After going through the Demo Day at Y Combinator with a solid presentation and the energy raring to go, picture investors showering you with love and money. Imagine feeling like the world is beneath your feet. Suddenly, everything feels conquerable. That's the point cockiness sets in and you are prone to making the most mistakes. It was enough hard work staying on top of all the hype and ensuring that things remain the way they were before the fame. On one hand, they were trying to keep their clientele happy while trying to grow their consumer base in the fastest way possible. So, it was imperative that they didn't ruin things.

While many startup founders tend to find themselves struggling to do all the work alone, inDinero has found that companies tend to prefer hiring an in-house accounting team or managing several different vendors instead of racking up wasted hours and thousands of dollars. InDinero positions itself as the perfect equivalent of, if not better than, an in-house team, but without the extra cost of having to manage in-house employees. The outfit takes care of all the stuff that presents a headache to business owners, such as bookkeeping, payroll, and taxes. They even provide clients with a designated success team that is regularly on hand to deal with problems and errors whenever they arise. Best of all, clients can be assured that their accounting services are performed by people who truly know and understand what entrepreneurship is like.

Jessica Mah tends to describe herself as an entrepreneur raised by entrepreneurs, with an entrepreneurial history of starting businesses since she was in grade school. Since she has a major in computer science from UC Berkeley, and another major in inDinero since starting the outfit in her dorm room with co-founder Su, clients have nothing to worry about. Mah understands that starting and developing a business is quite the monumental task, and believes that the more help a startup gets, the better its chances of success. Mah is even known to let in the competition on some of her trade secrets. In her words, what's good for the goose is equally good for the gander. She expressed a deep desire to help out friends and strangers who share her interest in entrepreneurship. Also, being in a relationship with an entrepreneur means that she naturally focuses her time and talents on people like her. So, for startup founders who feel like they are taking on too many tasks than they can manage, InDinero is willing and able to manage their accounting tasks for them. They don't even have to bother about it ever again.

Mah's approach to the business has been a real game changer. As of September 2018, InDinero managed to raise up to $10 million in equity finding while managing a roster of about 30 investors. Just before that, on May 8, 2018, the outfit acquired tempCFO, a firm based in San Jose. In the following year, on the first of February, 2019, InDinero procured its second company, mAccounting, a tax and accounting firm based in Indianapolis. Two years before their second procurement, InDinero ended the business year on a high, racking up $7.5 million in revenue, with a projection of ending 2018 on a revenue run rate of $22 million and staying EBITDA positive.

Another key feature in the fast growth of the company stems from their interactive web-based interface, which ensures the efficient management of the finances of clients' businesses. Users can access and analyze their financial reports from convenient explanations on their dashboard. InDinero also helps in preparing and filing tax returns for their clientele, as well other functions such as invoicing, generating reports, automating the categorization of financial transactions, and processing credit cards. Following a seamless integration with Trinet Ability, inDinero works with a team of experts to assess and analyze the revenue recognition and cash runway of client businesses. With Stitch Labs Detailed, inDinero is also able to prepare streamlined inventory management using visualizations of financial data.

Understanding the Future of Technology in Accounting

It'd be illogical to ignore the fact that the role of accounting in business has evolved since the introduction of technology into the practice. The mobile and digital landscape that many businesses live by promoted the adaptation of accounting in a bid to keep up with the big data environment of recent times. From historical patterns, it can be deduced that the role of accounting in business has always been relegated to reactionary and back office. In recent times, however, accounting has evolved to more than just an audit and tax function to a service that is both future-centric and advisory in nature. Additionally, CEOs now expect some level of data analytics skills and technological literacy from accountants.

The technology used in business accounting is constantly innovating, so it's imperative that CFOs and CEOs keep abreast with technological trends that could turn out to be game changers in the industry, and more importantly, for their business. In a 2018 study by AccountingToday, up to 50% of small, medium, and large-scale firms implemented accounting software in their businesses. In this new period of remote working and economic uncertainties, accounting software systems have been on an ever-increasing demand, some of which are:

1. **Artificial Intelligence (AI):** Many tend to accuse AI of devaluing human contribution to the field of accounting, but it remains factual that automating tasks that involve analyzing, recording, and collecting data helps to redirect manpower to accounting functions with higher values. According to a recent study, up to 85% of executives admit that their companies would be better off with AI. Savvy leaders comprehend how technological advancements

in AI like robotic processing automation help to create a competitive advantage, as well as the resources and expertise necessary to take complete advantage of AI accounting.

As accounting systems evolve in their use and implementation of artificial intelligence, businesses that latch onto these advances in technology will reap their rewards in matters such as easier and faster identification of anomalies for audit purposes, more sophisticated financial forecasting and predictive models, optimal operational efficiency, and better user experience with voice recognition software.

2. **Blockchain:** The increase in cloud accounting resulted in a corresponding increase in the adoption of blockchain for storing contracts and digital transactions safely and more transparently. In simpler words, blockchain is a list of digital records in the form of blocks, which are publicly stored as chains on several machines. Basically, a blockchain is the subset of distributed ledger technology. In the accounting industry, advocates for the adoption of blockchain technology, which includes the Big Four accounting firms, highlight the main features of its design. The chain is public (although transaction data is available to all,

private data remains encrypted), every transaction can be traced to its origin, all errors in data entry are entirely removed using automation, and it's impossible to corrupt the blocks. However, regardless of these features which are seemingly made for accounting, executives have dragged their feet in adopting blockchain solutions. In a 2018 study, four out of 10 executives blame government regulations for thwarting the process.

Regardless of the many barriers involved, the projected market spend of the blockchain market sat around $4.3 billion U.S. in 2020. According to IDC market analysis, early adopters of the process experienced higher benefits during the early periods of the COVID-19 pandemic. Additionally, growing partnerships such as the one between the nonprofit Wall Street Blockchain Alliance and the American Institute of CPAs will continue promoting the growth and adoption of blockchain solutions in the accounting industry. The level of confidence shown in the qualities of blockchain in accounting, as well as other industries such manufacturing, real estate, consumer goods, and healthcare, will doubtlessly keep the trend going for longer.

3. **Cloud Accounting:** C-suite managers and accountants alike value cloud-based software

due to its effectiveness and efficiency in business. There is a growing demand for both cloud-based accounting and on-premises software even though the trend inclines towards integrated (app and cloud-based) accounting software. With integrations, the ability of the cloud to scale without needing to use an expensive and time-consuming software implementation is unlocked. Only some years back, cloud-based accounting outfits forecasted revenue growth in double digits year in, year out, in comparison to the meager 4% growth of traditional accounting firms. Moreover, accounting firms are more willing to use cloud-based accounting, which is also a favorite among their client base.

According to analysts, the global cloud managed services market is projected to reach $115.6 billion U.S. by 2026, with an 11.6% CAGR between 2021 and 2026.

Other computing and technological innovations to watch out for:

As long as there are advanced in telecommunications and computer technologies, innovations in the accounting industry are to be expected. Some innovations that are worth considering now and in the future include:

- Intelligent Automation (IA)
- Quantum computing
- Robotic Process Automation (RPA)
- Edge Computing
- Fifth Generation (5G) cellular network technology

Things You May Not Know About Jessica Mah

1. In an interview with Jessica Mah, the inDinero founder admitted to prioritizing a good night's sleep. She expressed confusion at why people bragged about having little to no sleep at all, adding that it was a recipe for disaster. Mah believes that sleep deprivation could lead to low productivity and subpar decision making.
2. Jessica Mah featured in the 2012 documentary on young web dynamos in the United States and Europe at large, *The Startup Kids*.
3. Following the launch of InDinero in 2010, Jessica Mah's relationship with her co-founder, Andy Su, encountered a rocky patch. To nip the

problem in the bud, Su handed Mah an ultimatum, threatening to leave if the latter didn't attend a counseling session together. In the end, the two wound up at couples' therapy—a hilarious ending that would save their business and relationship as friends.

Things to Know as a Startup in the Accounting Industry

1. Think of job candidates like customers. First impressions matter everywhere else in life; the same goes for your potential candidates. You can work wonders to improve your external image, but if a potential job candidate's interaction with your brand falls short of those they've had with your competitors, then they are more likely to choose the company with whom they had the better experience. Job candidates, like your regular customers, expect some levels of hospitality and respect from you. They also expect to hear back from you on time about their applications. Based on a recent study carried out on applicants, 23% report losing interest in a position if an organization

doesn't get back to them within a one-week period.

Conversely, about 46% of candidates admitted to losing interest entirely if an organization doesn't get back to them within two weeks. These statistics go to show that it is imperative for your business to use diligence in maintaining regular communication with applicants to improve your chances of recruiting top talents.

2. Cater to the needs of job applicants. As the years roll by, the expectations and desires of job seekers tend to evolve. The current generation of applicants are usually on the lookout for more from potential employers than a regular paycheck—an evolution many employees are latching onto with a promptness. Now, companies are starting to offer better and more comfortable working arrangements for their workers. Although benefits coupled with a healthy salary are imperative, it's best to think outside the box. This will put your business in a different light that job seekers find attractive and will be more willing to work at, due to the unique perks you offer. Another method of attracting the new generation of workers is to express how their jobs could differ from similar roles at a different company.

When candidates find your business leveraging new and innovative technologies such as cloud-based systems that allow for remote working and automation of tedious tasks with business automation softwares, you improve your chances of attracting workers who are more likely to commit their time on the job, be more effective, and enjoy the process. Although it may appear like there are many different ways to set your business apart from others, it's necessary to understand that it's the little changes made over time that go a long way to attract the very best applicants now and in the future.

3. View your business from the perspective of an outsider. Businesses tend to focus on the internal processes of the outfit so much so that they give little to no thoughts on how a job seeker perceives them. It's one thing to offer great working perks like a decent salary and additional benefits, but if and when a potential job applicant goes on your webpage, what would their impression be? Would they find an outdated site that casts a shadow over the position you're offering and the company as a whole, or would it make them relish the prospect of working with you? This logic also applies in the event that your business has been the subject of negative reviews on sites such as Indeed, Trustpilot, and GlassDoor.

When looking to improve the external image of your business, consider the qualities you'd personally be interested in at a job and business you're applying to. With that in mind, assess the ability of your outfit to enact those qualities. Although it isn't entirely possible to prevent negative criticisms on job review sites, attempting to address and resolve negative feedback will set you on the right path. Potential job applicants will find that you are interested in the well-being of your workers.

Chapter 3:

Marketing

Whenever you buy an item, whether it's an online purchase or from a physical store, it usually begins with a need for or an attraction towards that brand or product. This leads to a series of decision making and change in interest (increase or decline) that will either cause you to abandon the purchase or buy the product.

This process is what marketers call a funnel. But, what if, as a business, you could monitor all of your marketing data in one place? This is the service provided by Funnel and one reason why the company has attained its present altitude.

Funnel can be used to collect data from every advertising platform, including social and non-social media, and arrange it comprehensively for the right eyes to evaluate. However, before Fredrik Skantze, the CEO of Funnel, struck gold with this idea, he too had lived through a business failure.

Born and raised in Sweden, Skantze would travel to America to study engineering and secure his Masters in Intelligence and Robotics at MIT. He returned to the US a few years later for an MBA at Stanford. Skantze made the decision to go to business school in preparation for starting a business sometime in the future. In his words, "I went to Stanford because I felt that, ultimately, I wanted to start a company."

Autoquake, a company founded by Fredrik Skantze (and his first), was established five years after he got his MBA. Before then, Skantze had worked for various big tech companies, gaining invaluable experience in both technology and business.

Autoquake started off on a good note, and seemed like it was on its way to becoming a well-established and hugely profitable business. Skantze and his partner were able to raise a $30 million capital, and their investors were excited about the business model. Autoquake was about selling used cars directly to consumers at a cheaper rate and giving part of the profits to the leasing companies. This model was so effective that the company grew by 500%.

But Skantze and his partner had gotten excited about the prospect and creating the next eBay that they invested more money than was safe into the growth of the company. Then came the 2008-2009 recession, and Autoquake staggered. They had been unprepared for this hurdle, and although they trudged along for a while, the business came to a close after six years of hard work and hope. A part of Autoquake was sold for less than they had imagined it would go for, and the other part was simply shut down.

This hit Skantze as hard as you might imagine it would for an entrepreneur who had put his knowledge, sweat, and various resources into building what should have been a successful venture. He recounts in an interview to Alejandro Cremades, a podcast host and author, "...it was a huge mind shift, and actually a bit hard to recover from..."

Thankfully, Skantze was able to learn from this setback, instead of writing himself off. Among the lessons he got from the failure of Autoquake was that he needed to spend more time figuring out the right market model, metrics, and how to scale a business.

All this happened around the same time when Skantze was having his first child. So, this was even more incentive to start a new business or go work for one. One could say that he did both. He went to work for a company that focused on marketing technology, where he found his Autoquake co-founder. They began developing a software that could be integrated with Facebook to help with advertising. They called this software Qwaya, and it was the lead-up to Funnel.

Funnel, like Qwaya, is a marketing software that helps people post and optimize ads on various online platforms. However, Funnel goes further to simplify the ad reports. That is, marketers and entrepreneurs don't need to be faced with complex spreadsheets. Instead, all the marketing data they need is presented in an easy-to-understand way. Users also do not have to manually input this data into Funnel. The software automatically collects data from every advertising platform employed by the user.

This proved to be a solution that people may have not clamored for (although answers from the surveyed customers of Qwaya ignited the idea for Fennel), but absolutely needed. Fennel quickly proved to be a winning idea, as it grew by about 150% every year. With this massive growth and the fact that the business model for Fennel was distinct from Qwaya, Skantze and his co-founder decided to do a pivot. This meant they introduced Fennel as a unique brand.

In some cases, a pivot can be problematic. For one, it is more expensive to promote a new brand or product than pre-existing ones. Although Skantze and his partner had the funds to keep Fennel running for a year, they didn't have enough to go beyond that. Another problem with a pivot is that your investors might be confused by the change in business direction. If even one investor loses faith in the new business, others could pull out too.

Fortunately, Skantze and his partner were able to surmount these challenges, and Fennel did not go the way of Autoquake. Their investors continued to believe in them, and they were able to secure all the funding they needed.

The growth of any business means that more hands will have to be hired. And with more individuals on board, there is the need for founders to organize their employees into effective teams. At this point, team culture must be introduced into the dynamics of the business.

The culture at Funnel is that the salespeople do not work individually for personal commissions. Instead, they have a project manager and collaborate. The sales team supports each other and shares ideas. This culture also goes for the development team and every other unit in Funnel.

Funnel is a good example of finding a gap in the market and creating the right puzzle piece. By perseverance and determination (more than a few people had essentially told Skantze that Qwaya and, eventually, Funnel was not solving any real problem), Funnel has risen to become the go-to marketing solution for some of the biggest brands in the world. In 2019, they hit an annual revenue of $10 million.

The best part is that Funnel is such a niche brand that it has no competitors.

Things You May Not Know About Fredrik Skantze

1. If he could go back in time and be 20 years old again, he would have tried starting a company in marketing technology instead of working for corporations. Even though his startup would be

small and, in the beginning, less lucrative than paid employment, he could be happy knowing he was doing something meaningful and impactful.

2. Skantze studies other CEOs of successful businesses to determine what they are doing right. He also applies what he learns from following these leaders into his own company. For instance, he studies the CEOs of HubSpot, Brian Halligan and Dharnesh, because of how they pivoted into CRM and their company culture.

3. He enjoys reading *Management 3.0* by Jurgen Appelo, a book that explains how managers can apply modern systems theory and software methodology to grow agile teams and lead better.

4. You might think that for someone who runs as successful a business as Skantze does, he wouldn't be able to get adequate sleep. But this is not the case. He's often able to get about eight hours of sleep every night.

However, in a 2015 interview with Samuel Villegas, Skantze admitted that maintaining a good work-life balance might be difficult at the early stages of a business. During this time, the entrepreneur is usually so focused on the survival of their company that adequate sleep and even spending quality time with family and friends may have to be sacrificed. Since such a lifestyle is unsustainable as it concerns physical, mental, and emotional health, entrepreneurs *should* make work-life balance a goal. They must seek out more sleep time as soon as their business takes off.

Things to Know as a Startup in the Marketing Technology Industry

If, like Skantze, you would like to break into the marketing technology (or martech) industry and dominate the market, then study and practice the tips below. They will improve your chances of success and give you an edge over both small and large competitors.

1. **Create a relationship with tech influencers**. It's a brave new world and these days, most marketing technology consumers rely on the reviews of their favorite influencers to make decisions. You can not only gain customer trust by getting good reviews from such influencers, but also learn about consumer needs that are yet to be met by the tech marketing industry.

2. **Timing is important**. Even though this means that you should provide the right tech solutions at the time it is most needed, you mustn't be so

focused on getting your timing right that you miss opportunities.

3. **Improve on existing technology**. Sometimes, you don't have to create something new. Never before seen and incomparable martechs are a rarity. The easiest and surest way to earn a piece of this industry is to determine the aspects that current technologies are lacking and how much a solution to this problem is needed.

4. **The technology should be functional and easy to grasp.** One of the biggest selling points of Funnel is that anyone, regardless of their knowledge on spreadsheets, data, marketing, or technology, can understand the reports. Since the data collection is also automated, this means less work for the end user.

   You can have a revolutionary product that people truly need. But if it is complex or doesn't always perform as advertised, then it is unlikely that your business will be successful.

5. **Your technology must fill a gap and be indispensable**. In other words, people have to *need* it. Wanting it isn't enough. And although there might be a cheaper alternative, your martech solution should be the most useful.

Chapter 4:

Female Entrepreneur

In commemoration of their first profitable month since opening, Lunya, the modern sleepwear makers, made a quiet donation to a new school for Girls Inc., which is a nonprofit organization that targets the girl child and helps them grow to be bold, smart, and strong. The school earmarked a new beginning in the chapter of the outfit—a moment Ashley Merrill had been expecting since she first founded Lunya with the aim of creating a systemic change for women. Since the launch six years ago, Lunya has donated an improved percentage of their revenue to Girls Inc., as well as hosting and volunteering workshops to impart girls on product development and business fundamentals. Part of Merrill's personal mission since her early years, when she struggled to find female role models to look up to, was advocating equal exposure and opportunity for young women in a variety of careers. According to Merrill, she grew up envisioning a future where she could have both a thriving career and a great family, but there weren't enough examples to pique her interest. While many might have looked away or lowered their expectations, the seed of an early calling had been planted in young Merrill, who sought to be the change she desired in the world.

She is a firm believer that businesses have a distinct capacity to advance the causes they cared about. With that in perspective, Merrill started Lunya with female empowerment as her goal and embedded it into every fabric of her enterprise. She began by creating best-in-class products and grew a business that creates opportunities for and uplifts women both within and outside of Lunya. Suffice it to say that Merrill's entire operation model revolves around a multifaceted approach to developing a business in service of women.

Following her graduation from UCLA, where she would return to bag an MBA, Merrill started a career in venture capital and online media. In 2012, she realized an opening to revamp the sleepwear market by developing a brand that was specifically created to cater to the lifestyle and needs of a modern woman. While their original offerings primarily revolved around traditional matching sets of lingerie, the intention of Merrill's brand is to create pieces that a woman picks for herself and feels confident in while at home. The rise of Lunya was fueled by its unique ability to mix inherent functionality and a signature aesthetic to create a new and exciting class of performance sleepwear. Lunya is a heavy investor in product development in a bid to ensure that every piece they make is not only embedded with feasible features that make it wearable in day-to-day life, but also with a design that flatters a woman's body.

The efforts of the brand in utilizing features, such as sourcing washable silk and alpaca wool and using breathable fabrics for the regulation of body temperature, continue to attract an increasing number of loyal customers. In March 2018, Lunya debuted one of their most pioneering collections called Restore. The line, the first of its kind, is a smart sleepwear that promotes and improves deeper sleep. With the new line, Lunya was able to enhance their natural Pima cotton using Celliant technology, a proprietary mineral mix under the regulations of the FDA, which has been clinically proven to improve the level of oxygen in the body. As such, cells undergo faster regeneration that aids you to wake up feeling more refreshed and energized. The team charged with the line developed a custom Restore fabric exclusive to the company, with plans to create and launch more transformational natural blends over time.

A Company Culture Designed to Uplift Women

Merrill was unmistakable about establishing the mission of her company to create a platform that uplifted women across all levels, including their employees, customers, and the community at large. According to her, it's only natural that a business like, hers founded on the grounds of improving the lives of women at home, would do that in every other way possible. Merrill believed that a business should be able to trace its mission across everything it's involved in. At Lunya, the process begins with empowering women leaders and promoting a culture focused on growth. The conscious effort of the founder to create a mission that women will feel inspired to identify with has attracted a team 82% dominated by women, with all the senior leaders of the brand being women.

According to Merrill, it isn't enough to create a business run by a woman. There's also a need to create a successful and thriving business. Only 2% of businesses run by women grow beyond the million-dollar mark, and only 3% of all businesses that went public in the last two decades have women as their heads. Merrill considers those stats disappointing and intends to do her part to improve the numbers. Many years after Lunya's inception, Merrill is still deliberate about continuing the collaborative culture of her business. She invests in the long-term growth and development of her team members and is supportive of their personal career ambitions. Lunya pushes its team members to undertake leadership roles by arming them with all the support and resources required to launch and succeed at new projects. Merrill also makes education accessible to its members, as well as professional events among other aids to help them grow in the same stride as the organization.

Lunya expresses an equal determination and dedication to the curation and production of a wide range of resources to elevate women in their respective communities. From creating events to content among others, the business constantly explored new methods of educating, congregating, and lifting women into the spotlight. Lunya hosts several different events monthly at its headquarters in Santa Monica, with a panel dedicated to busting motherhood myths, a workshop to improve career comebacks, and an event on financial planning, among others. It's Merrill's sincerest hope that the enduring impact of her brand will come in the form of Lunya's larger mission to aid women in breaking the cycle of penury in their families. Over the years since starting the company, Merrill has met with different organizations in a bid to find the major areas that Lunya can fill to shape a better future for women. According to Merrill, she went into Lunya hoping to find a silver bullet before discovering the interconnectedness of things. As a result, she realized the contributions of the company had to be interconnected too. In her words, "We don't want to hope that Lunya is making a difference for women. We need to see measurable change."

Merrill came to discover the three main obstacles that held women back, namely opportunity, health, and education. With this in mind, Lunya and its founder are now focused in different ways of supporting change in every domain possible. The company started by striking an education partnership with Girls Inc., where Merrill served as a board member. With more that 125,000 girls in coverage each year, Girls Inc. offers before, during, and after-school programs in the most underserved communities around the county. The impact of Girls Inc. is generational because it equips the female child with all the necessary tools required to enact changes in their family. By being the first of their siblings to go to college, they are presented with a getaway ticket to a different life and a holistic leg up in the foreseeable future.

Merrill went on to focus on family planning to ensure that women were only starting families they felt ready for. Disturbing statistics posit that up to 210,000 teenage girls have children annually, with only 40% of those graduating from high school and an even lesser 2% going on to graduate from college by 30 years of age or under. To cancel this disturbing culture, Lunya is an avid supporter of Upstream, which is a national organization dedicated to providing on-site training to healthcare centers. This training equips the centers to educate women and offer them a vast array of contraceptive methods.

In addition to investing in the continuation of education for young women, Merrill also aims to offer them support whenever they begin their careers or create their own ventures. This move is personal to Merrill, and stems back from her days in venture capital. The eureka moment fame for the generous founder at a local pitch competition where she was representing her venture capital firm at the time. A female entrepreneur took the stage to pitch her business ideas, which piqued the interest of a roomful of 60 middle-aged men. They turned to assess the pitch, even though the entrepreneur was no more than 21 years old with no knowledge whatsoever of investments. There and then, it became clear to Merrill than women needed more funding. And not just from anywhere, but from other women too, because they are more likely to relate better to the businesses created by other female entrepreneurs, as well as the consumer base the business hopes to serve.

To create such a systemic change, Merrill argues that more women with the fiscal capacity to propel businesses for success are needed. Women who have successfully built thriving outfits are also necessary, as they serve as a prime example to other women and as validation that women could rake in strong returns if invested in. In recent times, Merrill is heavily invested in businesses led by women, such as The Citizenry and Peek, and has functioned as a lending partner to Halogen Ventures, a female-led venture capital fund based in LA, which invests with a gender lens. Merrill's hope is that the women she funds now will go on to be successful enough to fund the next generation of women some 15 years from now.

In March 2018, to commemorate the International Women's Day, Lunya partnered with several brands owned by women, such as Vrai Oro, Jenni Kayne, and Janessa Leone, to donate a percentage of their sales to Girls Inc. Lunya went on to design a limited edition version of their much coveted muscle tee, donating 100% of all the proceeds. When Merrill reached out to Stofenmacher (founder of Vrai & Oro), Kayne, and Leone to talk about the idea of a donation, the resounding agreement of the women was symbolic of the fervor of the women movement. According to Merrill, "Our society is being driven by a community of women who want to see each other win. We advocate for each other and then we advocate for something bigger than ourselves. Every one of these women is constantly asking: How can I turn around and make the path easier for the woman coming after me? This is the change we have all been waiting for. The movement for women isn't just underway. It's happening, and it's happening fast."

Things You May Not Know About Ashley Merrill

1. Merrill owns another brand known as The Deep, which was formed in April 2019 in Santa Monica, California. The aim of the brand is to save humanity by pushing questions that stoke the curiosity of people about the world and those around them and giving them something to think about.

2. If the name Merrill sounds familiar to you, that's because Ashley is married to Marc Merrill, a popular businessman known for founding and chairing Riot Games, a game publisher and developer responsible for the hit franchise League of Legends.

3. Merrill's first-ever degree was a Bachelor of Arts from the University of California, Los Angeles (UCLA).

Things to Know as a Startup in the Sleepwear Industry

1. After returning from a hectic day at work, we all know that urge to get out of the cumbersome confines of work clothes, take a shower, and slip into more comfortable house wear. But wearing your house clothes isn't an excuse to look non-chic or dowdy. Comfort should not have to come at the cost of feeling good and looking your best. These were the exact thoughts of Ashley Merrill that led her to found Lunya. It all began when she took a casual look at the mirror and was surprised at her reflection. Never in a million years did she want to be seen in that way—as some woman who didn't care enough to look good. The women of today need a sleepwear that is reflective of their personalities as beautiful, chic, and modern. And that was exactly what Lunya came to be about. Ashley Merrill went from nightmare in a mirror to going out of her way to source the perfect sleepwear that combined beauty, comfort, and feasibility.

But her crusading came to a futile end as she couldn't find anything that ticked her boxes. So, she took the plunge and started the journey of creating the perfect sleepwear. Merrill set off on a mission to create a market that catered to the downtime of every woman with the perfect loungewear.

2. Design your team around several job functions. For Merrill, creating the perfect team revolved around taking a look at the issues in her staffing, analyzing the people already in her employ, and asking herself how to make things work. She'd soon get a paradigm shift that made her realize that her approach was wrong. Her new strategy is to analyze certain job functions and make informed decisions on who to hire, rather than pushing others into roles they're unequipped to handle. So, for instance, if there are 20 roles to fill (creative, product development, marketing, wholesale, finance, retail, and legal) but there are only four people at hand to cover these roles, instead of pushing these people into roles that don't utilize their core strengths, it's best to hire professionals.

3. As a woman's guide to navigating business challenges, Merrill posits a somewhat contrary view that being a female founder could be leveraged to your advantage in today's environment. According to her, it's a good period right now because there are executives

who only invest in businesses using a gender lens. Also, some segments tend to offer funding to female-run businesses, so her point holds. Sure, you have to have something to offer, but when you do, there are people out there specifically aiming to give you all the support you need.

4. Funding is often a tricky business. According to Merrill, funding isn't in short supply regardless of what it is that you intend to offer, given that the idea is solid and your business rakes in revenue. However, Merrill admitted concern to startups that begin with valuations that are through the roof. Raising funds isn't the most difficult part of creating a startup, it's the valuation that goes into the process. For instance, $20 million amounting to a $100 million valuation. In such cases, it's imperative that founders know that many investors are on the lookout for something around the range of a billion or half exit. Hence, it's critical to be real about what the market is for you and be invested in what your business would be about going forward. It's okay to set yourself up for an exit at a figure of several billions, but is your market capable of that or is it too saturated?

Merrill's advice to potential founders is to employ realistic thinking in assessing the potential of your business and your target market before accepting fundings at huge valuations. Your business could go on to be successful, but the success may not be worth several billions of dollars. You have to ensure that your investors would be satisfied with the same outcome you expect and are satisfied with.

5. Develop your brand through the perspective of your consumer base. When creating a startup, it helps to have a problem in mind which your business aims to solve. To do this, the perspective of your consumer base is imperative in building the company during its early stages. Your mind should be fixed on your target audience and how best to satisfy them. With that in mind, you'll be able to make informed decisions that shape the company culture and processes. It helps to remember that you aren't trying to solve everyone's problem. On how she improves her brand from the consumers perspective, Merrill and her team use fictitious people, whom they give certain histories, such as a job, children, hobbies, and age. These stats help with optimum clarity from the standpoint of branding to the creation of the product. It also helps them understand the disparities that could exist across their target consumers.

Merrill is an avid believer in this practice, admitting that it helps with clarity in brainstorming and problem-solving, as well as clarity of the unique voice of every customer— which is the best guide. Without this, you will end up barking up the wrong tree and targeting the wrong audiences.

Chapter 5:

Child Entrepreneurs

When one imagines a founder, it rarely, if ever, comes to mind that a child might fit into this category. This is because entrepreneurship is characteristically hectic. It is physically, emotionally, and mentally demanding. And, indeed, only the most persistent and resourceful survive.

These days, kids are proving that they too can compete with their much older peers and thrive. This was the case with a then 14-year-old boy named Robert Nay. He created a multi-level puzzle game that would replace Angry Birds as the number one free app on the App Store in 2011. Keep in mind that Angry Birds was designed by Jaakko Lisalo (40) and a corporation named Ravio Entertainment.

And while you might think that success in business, however small, is easier for young founders, this isn't the case. In fact, most of them are unable to win the confidence of investors because of their age—even when their ideas are good. They are seen as not having enough experience (which *is* true), and not being old enough to have the backbone that makes the best entrepreneurs.

However, one thing that young founders undeniably have is access to unlimited information. We're presently living in the age of the internet and social media. And, as you might have observed, millennials (1981-1986) and, especially, Gen Zs (1997-2015) are able to wield the power of both the internet and information better than their older contemporaries.

This is something that child entrepreneurs exploit in their favor. Robert Nay had not learned programming at some prestigious university or worked for a tech company before launching Nay Games. To gain knowledge on how to code, he visited his local library to do some research. Next, he asked his parents for money ($1200) to buy a new MacBook and purchase software licenses. One month later, and after more than 4000 separate lines of code, Bubble Ball was born.

The game proved to be a winner. Two weeks after it was uploaded to the App Store, it had over two million downloads. Although it was a free game, Bubble Ball showed that Nay had something appreciable and profitable to offer the world of gaming.

Once people were hooked on the free version of Bubble Ball, Nay introduced interesting updates—many of which were only available as pro versions of the game. This is a true display of Nay's business and marketing talents. Soon after the success of his first game, he established his own game development company called Nay Games.

As of 2016, Robert Nay had a net worth of $2 million.

Things You May Not Know About Robert Nay

1. Even though Bubble Ball had two million downloads in two weeks, Nay had not done anything particularly grand to promote the game. All he did was tell his friends and family members about it. Most of them already knew that he was developing the game.
2. He hopes to someday write an ebook that would help other people learn about iPhone game development.

Things to Know as a Startup in The Gaming Industry

1. Have as few barriers between your game and the consumers as possible. It should go with saying that if your brand is not yet popular, then your first game(s) should be entirely free. Also, if you can help people to play your game without the need to download it, this is a huge plus.

2. You should consider staying in school or not leaving your job, even when the game shows some initial promise. This is because while your game is free, you will not be making any income from it. And it might take some time to build your brand to such a height that you can add updates that players must pay for. In the intervening period, you will have to pay your bills and consider the fact that your game might not perform well enough for you to drop out of school.

3. If you have the resources to develop your game on multiple platforms, then it is best that you do so. Try not to give in to comfort and fall into the trap of putting all your eggs in a single basket. You can also make it available on Google Play and Facebook.

4. Grow a fanbase. Sometimes, people just need to see your excitement about your game before they try it themselves. There are also a large population of potential players who are yet to find out about your game. So, open social media accounts, create engaging posts, upload regularly, and run ads to build your online credibility.

You can also create a game within a game by rewarding certain players of your game for their loyalty or skill.

Chapter 6:

People of Color-Owned

Business

As a college student, years before breaking into the limelight with a stunning performance in Baby Boy (2001), Taraji P. Henson kept busy with wet sets at her home, which also doubled as her office. She charged $20 for her services, and had a loyal clientele who didn't mind the cost of looking their best. Henson would go on to be a regular on TV and movie sets for more than two decades, transforming into several characters with different iconic hairstyles to match her boisterous persona. With a seemingly great career, it's hard to imagine anything could go wrong. But it did. Henson suffered some damages to her scalp and hair with each hairstyle she made for the set. It didn't help that the market was oversaturated with products that promised a lot but failed to address the issue.

Tired of her increasing stash of products, Henson took matters into her own hands and attempted to create a solution of her own. She started experimenting in her kitchen to create a product that could provide her a healthy hair and scalp. Then, as a stroke of luck, it occurred to her that she couldn't be the only one experiencing such a problem. Henson went on to improve her experimental product, launching an entire line of hair products known as TPH by Taraji. She aims to develop into a huge haircare empire over the years. While her charm and talent on the big screens have gained Henson 32 awards among huge loads of nominations, this new chapter in her life has her returning to her first love. In her interview with *Allure*, Henson admitted to loving and understanding hair from her younger years. She grew to take her hair seriously, and never failed to show up at a salon every other week to change up her hairdo.

TPH by Taraji comes as the budding fruit of Henson's passion and dedication to hair over the years, which stemmed from personal experiences in styling and nurturing her own hair. The brand is also a result of a bit of trial and error that we all undergo in the process of learning to take care of our hair. The haircare line comes with 18 pieces that are categorized into four color-coded groups. Yellow represents products designed for scalp care, red is for hair and scalp repair, teal is for care and cleansing, and purple is for treatment stylers. According to Henson, the heart and foundation of TPH is scalp care, stemming from her experience of changing weaves across the gears.

She admitted to *Allure* that the first time she went to have a weave taken out, it had the smell of mildew, which gave the actress a case of embarrassment at the salon. She explained that although she washed her hair well enough, she didn't completely dry the weft. When an install or weave is being applied, hair is first braided down and then a hair net may or may not be sewn onto it. Next, the hair tracks are sewn onto the net or the braided hair itself. Once the weave or install was completed, the scalp would almost be impossible to reach. Henson found this process problematic, because she dreaded having the smell of mildew ever again. Her dread pushed her to make the Master Cleanse, which is a product inspired by her homemade concoction back in the day that she used to refresh her scalp whenever she wore weaves.

TPH by Taraji isn't made with a certain hair type in mind, and it isn't solely designed for those that wear weaves regularly. According to Henson, TPH caters for every hair regardless of its texture, whether it is fluffy or bone-straight or gravity-defying z-shaped zigzag strands or silky. When *Allure* attempted to test the product range on a variety of hair types, the difference was clear. They'd barely squirted out a lick when the quality of TPH presented itself. It's hard to judge a book by its cover, unadvisable too, in the same way a beauty product should never be judged by its packaging. But TPH was a dreamboat right off the bat. The products come in gorgeous packs that gave the impression of a luxury product.

In 2017, tired of all the work, efforts, and chemicals going into her hair, Henson cut all her hair and grew it back out as naturally as possible. She wanted a healthy head of hair with a curly pattern that matched all over, and she got just that. Afterwards, Henson swore off using heat on her hair, which was a very transformative period in her life. When she first began the TPH line, Henson's target audience were women that wore protective styles. But after losing her hair and growing it again, she broadened the range of the brand. The styling and conditioning formulas of the new products are intended to nourish and protect the hair from its tips down to the scalp. The new products were further influenced by lots of clients' feedback on Henson's Instagram, as well as her group chats and her personal wash day routine.

Henson now considers her wash days as part of her self-care routine, and has made it a point to treat herself regularly. The goal is to make the process fun and invest in taking care of herself. It's a bit like feeling down until you get up to take a shower, throw on some clothes, and apply some makeup. Then you start to feel good. To Henson, washing her hair makes all the difference because it impacts her disposition. However, in her journey towards creating the perfect self-care elements, Henson isn't solely focused on herself. In 2018, she created the Boris Lawrence Henson Foundation, which she named after her father, a veteran who returned from the Vietnam War suffering severe mental issues. The foundation is geared at breaking the stigma surrounding mental health management in the black community of the United States.

Besides that, Henson has a talk show on Facebook Watch called Peace of Mind With Taraji, where she discusses various subjects that are dear to her. Somehow, hair manages to entwine itself in her dealings again. Regardless of the legislation to tackle hair discrimination, the phenomenon is still quite rampant in workplaces and schools across the country, with black folks being at the short end of the stick. The CROWN Act, which was co-founded by Dove, pushes to make such a bias illegal across the country, but only seven states have passed the bill so far. In September 2020, legislation of the bill across the federation was approved by the House, however, it is yet to be voted on by the Senate. If everything goes to plan, Henson just might be on course to achieving success in two of the main things she holds dear: hair and the black community.

Things You May Not Know About Taraji P. Henson

1. Taraji P. Henson didn't always want to go into the theater. It might be surprising, but theater was a bit of a second thought for the illustrious actress. She started out pursuing a different dream entirely—engineering. While it might be difficult to picture Cookie Lyon in a hard hat and a bright orange jumpsuit, she did attend North Carolina Agricultural and Technical State University and the University of the District

Columbia, where she studied for a degree in electrical engineering.

2. She had a change of heart in regards to what she studied in school. Engineering was a tough dream for the young Henson, who started to struggle with the course. At some point, she got some clarity and pondered her decision to continue studying engineering. She'd failed pre-calculus and her math wasn't getting any better. In a final show of doggedness, Henson transferred to Howard University, where she settled for a degree in the performing arts.

3. Henson took on unusual jobs during her college years. While she breezed through her new life as a theater student, some things didn't fall into the most pleasant of places, particularly money. As a result, she had to juggle multiple jobs to see herself through school and not end up homeless. During the day, Henson worked in the Pentagon. That's correct, she worked at one of the most secure places in the United States. At night, she pulled up in a uniform and served as a waitress. But even that didn't get her all the money she wanted, so she put her singing skill to use by singing on a dinner cruise ship known as the Spirit of Washington.

4. She's a Golden Globe nominee. *Empire* is one of the biggest and well-received shows to hit the

big screen. And although the cast were A-listers and great in their own way, Taraji has stood out in her iconic role as Cookie Lyon. In 2015, the actress was nominated for the Golden Globe award in the category of "Best Actress in a Television Series Drama." It was her first time getting such a nomination since starting her career.

5. With the choice of Lucious, Henson proves right the point of surrounding yourself with the right people. When she was approached to play Cookie in Empire, Henson specifically agreed to the role on the condition that Lucious would be played by Terrence Howard. She claimed that she had great chemistry with the actor to play the dysfunctional couple and would rather Howard than anyone else. Fans of the show know that no one would have nailed down the role of King Lyon better.

Things to Know as a Startup in the Haircare Industry

1. Never underestimate the power of self-care. Before you build a brand to empower people to embrace themselves and express their beauty,

you first have to love and empower yourself. If you have the ability and strength to muster hate for someone, then you're quite capable of hating yourself. When you express true love for yourself, it's easier to learn to love others and show them how to love what you offer. Let's take Henson, for instance, when rumors were flying around that she had a face job to improve her looks. The rumors were untrue, because she was dealing with a health problem at the time that made self-care imperative for her. So, she took to working out and losing some weight.

Notice that her first modus operandi was to get her health back on track before addressing the rumors. Self-care was the more imperative route to take, not because her public image was under threat, but because she had to be there for herself first. Rumors come and they go, but a clean bill of health is something that cannot be understated. Treat your brand that way. Be more conscious of its longevity than you are about what people have to say about it. This doesn't imply that you should totally block out everything—criticism, praise, and whatnot. Just filter what gets to you and focus on yourself more.

2. Embrace what makes you different and learn from the uniqueness of others. Henson makes a solid point when she said in an interview that

we're on earth to look and sound different for a reason. Imagine if everyone looked and sounded alike. We'd all have the same stories and experiences, and nothing would be different—just stale and redundant. Lots of women before and after Henson may not have had problems switching between different hairstyles regularly, but the TPH founder did. And it's for that difference in experience that she now has a thriving brand that caters to people out there with experiences just like hers.

Your story may differ from other startup founders', and that's totally normal. You may not have an emotional and existential connection to your brand like Henson, but your drive and commitment is enough. It's okay to have a different driving force. Learn from others who've had different experiences, embrace your own uniqueness, and achieve even greater heights.

3. Surround yourself with the right people. Having the right type of company is an undersold quality. Henson would not have become as successful as she now is without some good company. She's testified that her friends couldn't care less about her public image as the almighty Cookie Lyon/Proud Mary. They call to check up on her regardless of her fame and

fortune without an underlying motive. It's this kind of people that push you forward. They could come as team members or friends and family members. With these people by your side, you could go on to be the next big thing because you know they've got your back. That's something you can't put a price on.

Chapter 7:

House Plant

Eliza Blank stands as proof that necessity really is the mother of invention. She came upon a personal need that, at the time, would not be easily met. And she resolved to provide the right solution.

Blank's journey to establishing The Sill began when she traveled to the ever-bustling New York. She had moved there to attend NYU and was quite excited by the change of environment. She felt ready for this change in part because her brother attended the same school. He was proof that she could survive the fast-paced city of New York, and his proximity to her was comforting. His achievements and presence would continue to inspire Blank, to the point of getting her to become a successful entrepreneur.

She studied communications in NYU, which is an asset in any business. As far as Blank's business background goes, she often recounts her brother's entrepreneurial spirit and her job at a hair care startup as being her biggest influences.

Her brother was a risk taker, but they were informed risks and he was always so dedicated and persistent that things always turned out right. This encouraged Blank to think about taking risks too. The idea for The Sill popped into her mind while she was in the university. Although she wasn't exactly afraid to take on the challenge of being an entrepreneur, she didn't know how to execute the business idea she had.

This particular problem, properly executing an idea, affects many would-be entrepreneurs. The issue of brand identity, raising capital, and knowing your customers well enough to target the precise demographic must first be sorted out before the entrepreneur presents their idea to the larger world. By working for the hair care company, Blank learned a few things that would make her the successful business person that she is today.

For instance, she discovered that she loved (and still does) hard work. In a 2017 interview with *Bird*, she describes herself as being nearly addicted to working. And guess what most successful entrepreneurs have in common: they have an incredible stamina, and often love, for hard work. She also learned business modeling and the disadvantage of raising capital before knowing as much as possible about one's business. Indeed, Blank gained invaluable knowledge by merely working for and studying the various businesses she worked for before starting her own. She would decide that having a niche was better than competing in a large market, and that consumer experience was the most important factor for longevity in business.

So, when it was time for Blank to start her own business, the idea would come in the form of a market that has been misrepresented and, for the most part, ignored: house plants. It is commonly believed that the customers of the house plant industry consist mainly of old women who live alone. And since there aren't many old, lonely women who need house plants, many entrepreneurs might be opposed to going into this industry.

As Blank realized, the problem wasn't with the industry itself, but the image it had. House plants, without the false branding, are simply beautiful and healthy. People who want to purchase plants for their homes and offices include all ages and genders. The house plant industry was, in reality, a large market. And Blank was ready to dominate it.

Besides the fact that people believed that only old, lonely women were interested in house plants, other problems that Blank had to contend with included:

- The arrangement of the plants
- Maintenance of the plants
- The aesthetics of the pot
- The readiness of the plant

By solving these issues, Blank believed that she could provide more value to her customers, beyond merely selling house plants.

When Blank was ready to start The Sill, she drew up a business plan and started a Kickstarter campaign. She chose Kickstarter as a way to not only raise money for the business, but also validate her idea. The campaign worked, which reassured her that The Sill would be solving a real problem. Blank and her co-founder, Gwen Blevens, who was excited enough about the house plant idea to leave her job, were able to raise $10,000. The Kickstarter campaign easily raised $12,000, which had been Blank's goal. With money from other sources, the total starting budget added up to about $32,000.

In the beginning of The Sill, there were just two employees. Erin was the marketing manager and PR, and Blank handled everything else. They worked hard and took every order they got with great care and professionalism. At this point, they were averaging about three orders a week, but there was never a week where they didn't make any money.

When The Sill got off the ground, the next hurdle for Blank was hiring the right people to increase the efficiency and productivity of her startup. This was scary for her because it can be hard to individuals who will be as interested and passionate about any business as the founder(s). Still, it has to be done if the business will continue to grow. She told *Bird* that The Sill had expanded to accommodate fifteen employees. Although these workers understood her story and shared her desire to help people beautify their homes with plants, Blank admitted that she was still scared to not only delegate, but also hire new hands. However, this kind of worry is trumped by the desire to see her vision for The Sill come to life.

Blank knew that besides good consumer experience, connecting with good suppliers ensures that businesses not only survive, but also stay competitive. In regards to how hardworking Blank is, seeking out plant suppliers was one of the most physically tasking challenges that she had to undertake. Speaking to *The Helm*, Blank remembered attending the Tropical Plant Expo in Florida and questioning a few distributors about the plant supply chain. She would take what might have been 12-hour walks, both in Florida and New York, to figure out where the growers and distributors are and meet with them.

She decided to get her plants from local growers, but she only purchased them after customers placed orders. Doing this saved her money in terms of inventory and maintenance. The planters, she bought ahead of time from ceramicists in New York. The Sill still operates by this model today.

Eventually, many businesses with more than one founder have to confront the challenge of one partner leaving the company. Since The Sill was originally Blank's idea, it was Gwen who chose to leave when they could not resolve their disagreements on which direction the business should move in. And like most legal unions, the dissolution of this business partnership was by no means a walk in the park. It had to be a win for both parties involved, with Gwen getting financial compensation for her initial investment. Gwen was also given a share of the company. The legal fees were, as expected, quite expensive, and this set Blank back a bit. Thankfully, she was able to bounce back from this, but it took some time.

By 2014, it had been two years since The Sill was run solely by Blank, and the revenue was not promising. Although profits were consistent, which is often a marker for targeting the right audience, there just wasn't any real growth. One reason for this might have been that Blank was thinking small. She recalled setting financial goals for the company and consistently hitting them. But she now realizes that the milestones she passed with ease were particularly small ones.

One might consider this from a different perspective and reason those small goals may be why The Sill remains in existence and continues to thrive. Although the company did not expand as quickly and in the manner Blank might have imagined, those small goals were enough to keep her excited and appreciative of the process. She also gained entrepreneurial experience that prepared her for major growth in the future.

It was around 2015 that things began to change for The Sill. The progress that Blank had hoped for would come in the form of unexpected B2B sales. Vine, which was a major social media platform during that time, reached out Blank to beautify their office spaces with plants. After Twitter bought and shut down Vine, they too contacted Blank to outfit their office with plants. Even though she had not envisioned The Sill as a B2B company, this new direction was especially lucrative.

She continued to grow her direct-to-consumer sales, but was able to double her cash flow by selling directly to business.

At this time in 2015, The Sill had been in business for almost three years, and Blank still wasn't paying herself. She subsisted on her savings and offered consultation services. She put everything she had into her house plant business and was content with living frugally. She had learned from her brother that a never-give-up spirit almost always precedes success. And she was willing to do all it took to make sure that she remained in the game.

With more money coming in, Blank was able to increase the size of her team. She looked for people with diverse skill sets who believed in her vision. She hired talented photographers who took professional pictures of her plants for platforms like Instagram and Pinterest. She also needed people to water and prune the plants before they were sent to offices and homes, so she got people to do this job. The Sill's now much larger budget even allowed for paid interns.

In the same year, Blank moved the company from her brother's office to a small space in Chinatown. The new 100-square-foot space, inadequate as Blank thought it was for her now growing business, served The Sill quite well. As small as it was, raising money to secure the space was not easy. She had to pay $3,000 a month and the lease was for three years. She eventually paid for the space, with her mom serving as the guarantor. Afterwards, there wasn't enough money to productively run the business. So, Blank went to TruFund to take a loan of $80,000. She had tried to get a loan from other organizations, banks included, with no success. But her company and its location fit the type that TruFund supports. She judiciously invested the loan into her business and, soon after, The Sill was shipping houseplants nationwide.

Although B2B continued to account for the greater percentage of her revenue, she hoped that she could return to what was her original vision for The Sill: direct-to-consumer sales. To bring this dream to life, it was clear to Blank that she had to reach out to venture capitalists for an investment. What worried her about this decision was that investors might not take The Sill seriously. For one, the house plant industry was not known to have an appreciable market share or customer base. Also, as big as her company had grown, it still hadn't surpassed $1 million in revenue. To bolster her own confidence, Blank decided that she would first increase her company's revenue before raising venture capital. This way, the investors could be sure that The Sill, with Blank in charge, was a true goldmine.

Her company's revenue for 2016 did surpass this milestone and, in 2017, Blank reached out to investors. The Sill had been doing so well for such a long time that she had already attracted the attention of a few people. Andrew Mitchell, the founder of Brand Foundry Ventures and an angel investor, was willing to have a stake in The Sill before Blank even met with him. Within a few months, Blank was able to meet with and secure investments from a few more venture capitalists.

By October of that year, she had raised $2.5 million in seed round funding. Her company was now ready for its next level of growth. The Sill stopped functioning as a B2B company and focused entirely on gaining new customers. They were now able to properly market the business, sharpen their targeting, and acquire more long-term customers. Even better, Blank was able to settle her TruFund debt and finally pay herself. Her first salary as the founder and CEO of The Sill was $60,000.

Her series A round turned out to be far more difficult than raising seed capital. The Sill had proved to be sustainable, consistently profit earning, attractive to consumers, and scalable. But there was a new challenge for Blank to overcome: leading a company while pregnant. She had no idea what her potential investors would think about a pregnant business leader. But she wasn't alone in this struggle. Courtney Favreau, who was the first on her series A round, was also pregnant at the same time as Blank. They would, in fact, give birth only a week apart. Blank's worries proved to be unfounded, as her investors were quite understanding. She also remained as competent as she had been pre-conception.

Favreau, who could relate much better with Blank, would often let the lactating mother use the executive room to pump breast milk. The series A funding would raise, in total, $5 million.

Blank's journey as an entrepreneur is proof that the best skills in business are built with time and experience. She had now become resilient, resourceful, and a problem solver such that even when faced with the challenge of the COVID-19 pandemic (like most brick and mortar businesses), The Sill was able to utilize e-shipping and not only remain afloat, but also stay competitive.

Things You May Not Know About Eliza Blank

1. The idea for The Sill came to Blank when she was 21 years old. It would take five years for her to gain enough business experience and funding to start her company.
2. She wakes up by 6:30 a.m. every day, except for Saturdays and Sundays.
3. In 2017, she had a personal collection of 30 plants.
4. She enjoys listening to podcasts, especially *How I Built This*.
5. Her self-care ritual involves getting the right amount of sleep, hiking, and doing yoga.

Things to Know as a Startup in the House Plant Industry

1. **Invest in plant photography.** As beautiful as the idea of improving the aesthetic of one's place with plants might be, it's not realistic to expect people to be driven to make a purchase by merely visualizing this improvement. Your customers need to see the magic of your plants with more than their mind's eye.

    To achieve this, you must be open to having a professional and talented photographer on your team. It helps if you explain your vision to them, so that they can capture the essence of both the plants and your brand.

2. **What's the current plant hype on social media?** If your business is out of touch with what is trendy, then there is a much higher chance that you will not reach as many customers as you need to be profitable.

    You need to find out which plants and arrangements are outdated and stay away from those. Figuring out what is trendy is also relative to your demographic. People in their twenties are often interested in styles and aesthetics that differ from those who are in their forties.

3. **Pricing will make or break your business.** You've probably heard this said before, but pricing your products too low is just as (or even more) dangerous as setting the price too high. You want to be taken seriously, but also affordable.

   Your pricing should reflect all the work that has gone into the product and be competitive.

4. **Be prepared to spend time searching for the right plants**. Once you know your demographic and have decided on price range, the next step is to find the plants that fit your goals. This is often not as easy as you might expect.

   Like Eliza Blank, you might have to visit a number of growers before you find the right plants. Remember to not give up, even if it takes a few weeks. You should also be willing to ask a lot of questions, as the answers might point you in the right direction.

5. **You must ship right.** This includes the speed of your delivery and how the plants are packaged. Some entrepreneurs believe that getting the product right and paying for ads are

all they need to have a successful business. While those are important factors, seemingly small things like getting the shipping experience right can make or cripple any business.

In fact, shipping is an effective way to improve customer loyalty and get word of mouth started. As such, it is imperative that your packaging is thoughtful and professional, and that orders are promptly delivered.

Chapter 8:

Edtech

Sandra Oh Lin had stumbled on the idea for KiwiCo without initially recognizing the treasure filled cave for what it was. When she realized the potential of her idea, however, she was prepared to give all she had to bring it to life.

Playtime for Lin as a child had involved hands-on creativity. As a working mom, she wanted a way to not only keep her children entertained, but provide them with a way to improve their creativity and problem-solving abilities. Through her own ingenuity, she put together small science experiments and analytical projects to keep her kids busy. Soon, her friends got interested and wanted their kids to be in on the fun. They also encouraged her to pursue these projects as a business, as it could be of immense help to busy parents.

At the time, Lin was managing the fashion side of eBay. So, one couldn't confidently say that KiwiCo started as a cash grab scheme. She did the market research, but also gave the idea of entrepreneurship and helping kids with STEM projects serious thought. As is evident now, she took the advice of her friends and launched KiwiCo.

If there is one lesson that an aspiring entrepreneur should take from Lin's brand, it's that the path to business success isn't by merely selling products. One should also be able to convince their customers about the value of and the solutions provided by the product. It is important that your products make people *feel*, as opposed to being another thing on a shelf, an alternative, or a fad. And to achieve this, entrepreneurs must be the first to be excited about their products.

Lin could see how her STEM boxes helped children and their parents, and she was able to communicate this to both her investors and customers. KiwiCo, according to Lin, doesn't just produce toys that children can be fascinated by. In fact, it is a way to spark the hidden genius in children and prepare them to be capable adults in the future.

Job opportunities and the world as a whole are subject to constant change, and only those individuals who can easily adapt will thrive in such an uncertain system. As such, even though STEM is an acronym for Science, Technology, Engineering, and Mathematics, the subscription boxes made by KiwiCo go beyond these fields to inspire artistic creativity, logical reasoning, and, ultimately, mold the confidence of young children.

Lin had built some entrepreneurial muscle from watching her folks work. Although her parents' business was nowhere close to the size of the company that Lin would manage, her first lessons on sales and inventory came from helping her parents with their kiosk that was set up in a local mall. She developed an interest in science and would study chemical engineering in Case Western Reserve University. She graduated summa cum laude and, after a few years, proceeded to get her MBA from Harvard. She gained real business experience from working for large corporations like Procter & Gamble and what were, at the time, startups like eBay and PayPal. She was handed the responsibility of managing teams of various sizes at these establishments—a skill that is invaluable to every founder.

All these meant that Lin was and is well-rounded as a business person. She has the risk appetite and energy needed to excel as an entrepreneur, and she is equipped with practical experience and knowledge to ensure that she is unstoppable. Her entrepreneurial endowments proved effective after KiwiCo was founded.

Lin raised venture capital in three rounds and was only able to get a relatively small $10 million. But this was enough for someone as competent as Lin, who also served a product that consumers needed. KiwiCo was established in 2011, and seven years later it was not only immensely profitable, but debt free too. In 2018, Lin's company made a staggering $100 million in profits from crates. Presently, the company has 100 employees, out of which about 70% are female.

Despite the growth of the company, Lin is still focused on making her products safe for kids and affordable for their parents. To this end, she has actual rocket scientists, mechanical engineers, and designers putting in their 1000 hours of work to come up with the best STEM products for their customers. A few times each week, children of different ages (from toddlers to teenagers) are invited to try out KiwiCo's latest products. This is one more vital step in ensuring consumer satisfaction.

As for how Lin promotes her brand, word of mouth is her preferred type of advertisement. She uses social media ads sparsely and relies on her customers being so impressed with her products that they encourage their friends and family members to choose KiwiCo. With the customer being at the fore of Lin's company, it is little wonder that the business grows by more than 65% each year.

Things You May Not Know About Sarah Oh Lin

- Although a widely successful woman, a typical day in Lin's life is quite similar to most parents who work. After preparing her kids for school and getting them there, she heads to work to lead her company. Lin often returns home early enough to have fun and bond with her children (she might play soccer with them). Then, she prepares them for bed—a task that often includes telling bedtime stories.

- Maintaining a good work-life balance is much easier for Lin than most entrepreneurs. This is because her kids understand and use the products that she sells. She is able, in a sense, to bring work home to engage her children.

- For Lin, her most virtuous habit is gratitude. She is aware that many entrepreneurs would be able to achieve her current level of success if they have the same opportunities as she did.

Things to Know as a Startup in the Edtech Industry

1. There are some industries where it might be fine to come in with your own version of the same project. For instance, if you are thinking about producing customized t-shirts, it might be as easy as finding out the latest slang and trend. But this is not the case in the edtech sector. Parents are particular about what their kids play with and learn from. As such, your products have to positively impact the market or your potential customers will stick to tested and trusted brands.

2. You must be able to prove that your products work to get investors and new customers interested. It is not enough to tell them that your brand is revolutionary. Instead, you are expected to show it to them. This could mean getting kids to test your products and, if necessary, having investors and parents watch. If you can prove that your product positively affects creativity and intellect—while keeping the kids entertained enough for their parents to engage in other activities—then you might just have a chance in the edtech market.

3. Before presenting your products to potential investors, ask yourself if the brand is scalable and can be considered disruptive. Discussing this with your team members can help you arrive at an accurate conclusion. There are a lot of edtech startups, but investors are willing to back those brands that are sure to cause a ripple (or more) in the sector. This could be because such a brand is utilizing technology that other companies are unaware of, or they have changed the status quo of STEM learning, for instance.

   If your startup is, indeed, disruptive, then you must figure out if it is also scalable. You want to grow in both your offerings and profit margin as a company. The profits, especially, are the most attractive aspect of any business to investors.

4. Before you invest a dime into the business, do your due diligence. Again, there are a lot of edtech brands, and you want to know how and where you fit in. Your research should highlight gaps in the sector and parts that need improvement. One benefit of carrying out such market research in the edtech sector is that you don't have to look far to find participants for your case study. You can use parents and kids in your family and friends circle. That is, of course, if the circle is wide and honest enough, such that interviewing and observing them helps you with a near accurate statistic of the larger market.

Chapter 9:

Health Care

Christopher Walker's entrepreneurial spirit stemmed from a personal journey, in which he sought to make an impact in the lives of other people. This desire would not come until Walker had first-hand experience of a health crisis, which compelled him to pursue natural health products as a line of business. His inspiration to develop UMZU into the biggest and most trusted natural products company around the globe came from Walker overcoming a brain tumor in his younger years. As he grew older, he discovered that there were millions of people struggling with chronic health issues that the traditional medical establishments couldn't help them with. Instead, these people get caught in an insidious loop of consuming drugs, whose side effects lead them to consume even more drugs.

Walker has shown a dogged determination to make a positive impact in different ways, particularly by educating people on the truths of health in the human body. He goes on to empower people with natural products that work in line with the body to improve and restore their life and vitality. Walker's passion for health started in the most unusual way. When he was hospitalized and doctors found a tumor in his brain, he refused regular treatment, instead deciding to work on himself. Walker took an alternate route, relying on natural medicines to help him recover from the tumor. He was only 19 at the time of the discovery, and the tumor was lodged in his pituitary gland. Walker couldn't bring himself to undergo surgery or take meds, which were more dangerous than they were helpful.

Within about 18 months of the diagnosis, he was able to overturn his health and become symptom-free. His only treatment was lifestyle adjustment, exercise, nutrition, and strategic supplementation. When he achieved success healing himself through natural means, Walker found a burning desire to share his experience with others. And so began UMZU, which he founded with his business partners Mike Dobson and Darren Crawford. As of now, Walker is a success story in the world of e-commerce, where he sells his health products. One could say his success can be traced back to his ability to be a self starter. It's commonplace to see entrepreneurs searching for too much money from external sources without first searching within for what they need to begin their own brand.

This culture is problematic for Walker, who is a firm believer in self-funding. He believes that entrepreneurs should only approach the possibility of creating a startup with the intention of funding the business themselves. He believes that too many entrepreneurs have been caught by the glam of the false ideation that taking capital from external sources to start up a business is ideal. Walker posits that not only does such a mindset hinder their creative abilities, but it so often results in blatant failure too. He recounts having one such experience, when his first business failed and he was so bankrupt he had to put up with living in his car in Brooklyn, New York. Every day, he would get up early and prepare for job hunting. He walked into Manhattan to take interviews and meet with people, all to no avail. The UMZU founder is thankful that he never landed any of the jobs he applied for, claiming it gave him a sort of perspective.

Walker pondered and came to the conclusion that the best he could do with his living conditions was to become scrappy and throw himself into learning and developing important skills. This decision paid off, as Walker was able to build himself back up until he was on his feet again. But he didn't stop there. In pursuit of longer lasting success, he founded the UMZU brand, which is responsible for helping more than half a million customers with its product. To prevent people from suffering a similar fate, UMZU creates free educational content for women and men across the globe. Following UMZU's success, Walker embarked on a new series of projects, which includes expanding the product line of the products offered by UMZU. In line with the new projects, Walker and his team created an app that helps to improve the customer service experience of consumers with their products.

In September 2020, Walker noted that the biggest goals of the company included creating a new dog supplement treat line, creating a line of natural 'thermo' foods, expanding their product line with new and improved supplement formulas that addressed the needs of consumers, and creating home cleaning and personal care products. The company experienced a rapid subscription growth in the past year, which opened it up to different ways of achieving its ultimate vision of creating healthier alternatives for each area of the daily lives of consumers. With the launch of the new UMZU mobile app on Android and iOS, the brand plans on launching a new online fitness platform by September known as UMZUfit. At the same time, Walker teased about his new book *How To Eat*, which is due to be released in January 2021. The book contains details about Thermo Diet principles and demystify some mainstream myths on health.

Even after getting his life together, Walker never believed that UMZU would grow into such a big, mainstream brand. But even now, not everyone knows of the company and the amazing products it offers, and Walker is determined to change that. In 2015, the brand became a registered company, which formulated and developed natural supplements of the highest quality possible. All its products have the backing of scientific studies and ingredients from clinical trials on humans. Furthermore, they are correctly dosed for people to use in providing their bodies with all the nutrients necessary to begin the process of self-healing. Walker is proud of his brand, which has gone on to help hundreds of thousands of lives since its inception, enabling many of them to avoid the dangerous meds peddled by pharmaceuticals and switch to natural and well-formulated supplements.

Walker admits to international dealings of the brand, stating that UMZU catered to consumers all over the world, with products shipped from their facilities based in Boulder, United States. He posits that it's only the beginning for the bigger and better things to expect from the brand. Walker has a dream to further develop UMZU into the top player in the natural products industry in the world with help from his business partners and amazing team members. Being a popular figure, Walker is obsessed with knowing and comprehending the truth, which he hopes for his audience to see in his writings and videos. He believes that there are no sacred vows in terms of telling apart fact and fiction, especially when it involves a subject as critical as your health.

The UMZu founder describes his journey into the healthcare industry as fun and rewarding, since he was able to take over the reins of his health at a younger age. With discipline and a positive mindset, Walker has successfully channeled his experiences and successes, as well as his love for knowledge into helping people achieve the best state of health possible. His belief is that health is critical to optimum performance, and the present conventional health paradigm isn't helpful to anyone.

Things You May Not Know About Christopher Walker

1. Christopher Walker stands at a staggering 1.93m (6' 4"), and might just be the tallest entrepreneur covered in this volume.
2. Christopher Walker has made a couple of appearances on the big screen, starring in movies like *Hickock* and *Senior Entourage*.
3. In the history of the program, Walker was the first ever student at Duke University to graduate from neuroscience in three years.
4. Besides UMZU, Walker also founded and co-founded other brands like Kinobody and Truth Nutra.

Things to Know as a Startup in the Health Industry

1. Embrace the possibility of failure. As an entrepreneur, it's imperative for you to come to terms with the reality that your startup could crash and burn. Healthcare startups aren't immune to failing, and may even be riskier than

other ventures. That's because the world of healthcare is as complex as they come. In some parts of the world, the recipients of healthcare aren't necessarily the ones funding the process. In other parts of the world, the system differs. This means that physicians and hospitals may rely heavily on fee-for-service revenue. Moreover, even if one decides to adopt a different method, the process would be slow due to the loss of revenue likely to occur in the short term. There's also the possibility of the bottom line being negatively impacted. As such, the likelihood of the medical community adopting any solution that may reduce utilization even slightly is low.

2. Pinpoint early themes during the starting process. It's easy to get caught up in the process and pay no attention to important cues. Sure, your idea may be solid and play out well theoretically. You may have even gotten a team behind you and received executive approval from stakeholders to begin the sales process. But then comes the problem: a few meetings later and no one seems to have gotten the hang of what you're on about. All of a sudden, it feels like you brought a doorknob to an orchestra as your instrument of choice. What was that about healthcare loving innovations, again? Truth be

told, your product isn't bad. Your ideas are good too. But your pitch fails to satisfy the clinical, financial, and strategic needs of your audience. Either that or you have failed in your attempt to clearly convey your vision and how your startup could go on to improve or meaningfully aid the solution of a problem that bothers the healthcare industry.

3. Create well-defined terms of partnership. As a startup founder, you must acknowledge how important achieving a new partnership deal is. There is a need for flexibility, as you're still a tiny setup wading in an ocean run by bigger, bureaucratic institutions with lots of legal representation. Avoid time wasted on debating term sheets. It's unimportant whether or not it's nonbinding. Instead, turn your attention to discussing and agreeing upon a high-level main structure before proposing a draft of your master services agreement and definite agreement with all the glitz and glam you can muster. It's going to be a long road, so gear up and set your sights on closing the deal.

Chapter 10:

Emerging Businesses

When Jonathon Barkl, Scott Fitsimones, and Chelsea Border started attending Arizona State University, they had no idea that they would soon be dropping out of school to manage a business that is now worth millions. They had not, in fact, been looking for a business idea at all. They stumbled on a good one instead, and it would forever alter the course of their lives.

Like many universities in the world, ASU did not have enough parking space to accommodate both its staff and students. As a result, a lot of students were forced to buy expensive parking permits. Students who could afford these permits paid as much as $1000 every school year. Even with this price, the parking space was so far away that they had to walk for about 15 minutes to get to school.

In trying to find a way to save money and avoid the needless stress of walking long distances to school, Fitsimones arrived at a solution. Instead of paying for permits, he would rent parking spaces from homeowners who were in close proximity to the school. And it worked as he had imagined. He approached homeowners and asked them if he could rent a portion of their parking space. Eventually, for the whole school year, Fitsimones only had to pay $80 to park his car. This meant that he saved 92% of his earlier spending on permits. And the walking distance to his school was merely a stroll.

This little hack would prove to be such a helpful solution to a lot of people that it evolved to be the successful company that it is today. In 2017, they kicked off the business and began helping students find available and nearby parking spaces. But at that time, they were only dealing with homeowners who did not mind making some extra cash by renting out space in their garages. After a while, however, it was clear that this model was unsustainable. There just weren't enough homeowners and driveways relative to the students who needed parking spaces. So, Fitsimones, Barkl, and Border went to certain organizations like local businesses and churches, and convinced the owners to rent out their parking spaces.

One thing these three young entrepreneurs had going for them, and something that up-and-coming business people can learn from, is the fact that they weren't greedy or hasty in their desire for money. They cared more about adding value to the lives of their customers and growing their startup, than trying to make a lot of money in the shortest possible time. So when they expanded their company to include the parking spaces of other businesses, they allowed these partners to join without providing a sign-up fee. They also gave 70% of the profits to their partners. Indeed, they were savvy enough to know that taking only 30% from a lot of partners would add up to more profits for their company than taking, for instance, 40 or 50% from only a few partners.

When 2018 came around, Fitsimones, Barkl, and Border were serving 250 parking spaces. They were so trusted that one church had given them 65 parking spaces. At this point, it was clear that the young entrepreneurs were in business. However, since it is impossible to successfully juggle a business of this scale and schoolwork, the founders had to decide if they were going to let their business go or drop out of school. It was, as it often is, a tough decision. After all, one can argue that there is more certainty and security in having a degree than betting on a startup, notwithstanding the fact that startups are, statistically, likely to fail.

They bet on themselves, dropped out, and launched AirGarage as a full-fledged business. The trip immediately began to bring in more property owners and grow their startup. The way AirGarage now operates has changed a lot since it was established. The model is now more complex—albeit comprehensible to both drivers and property owners—and effective. The company now boasts of a skilled network of parking agents, to make sure that no driver gets away with illegal parking. This is one less thing for the parking lot owners to worry about.

Partners with AirGarage can also set the availability of their parking spaces, which protects them from intrusion. The company utilizes technology to further ensure safety and efficiency by placing cameras at the entrances of every parking lot that has registered on its platform. Every vehicle that enters an AirGarage will be scanned, and the time of parking and departure will be registered in the company's database. This compels drivers to pay in full to continue enjoying this valuable service.

The process of finding an AirGarage is also quite simple for customers. All they have to do is look for available spaces on the website, follow the instructions they receive to sign up for a guest account, and drive to the parking space to complete the registration and secure the space. Returning customers do not have to go through this slightly time-consuming process. The system recognizes them, and they can quickly pay for their space.

When the trio raised venture capital, they were able to secure an investment of $2 million. They now have registered parking lots in 22 states in America, and some more in Canada. AirGarage currently makes a yearly profit of about $1.6 million annually.

As with the other businesses discussed in this book, the then 23-year-old students who founded AirGarage discovered a problem and provided a solution. They did not attempt to invent a new niche or force a new product on consumers, which is what a lot of entrepreneurs think will make them billionaires.

Things You May Not Know About Fitsimones, Barkl, and Border

- The founders of AirGarage don't mind hiring seniors, and they also delegate work to willing and competent family members. For instance, Jonathon Barkl's dad helps out at AirGarage. This is not to say that they encouraged nepotism. But in the case of Barkl's dad, he is cheap, willing, and loyal labor, whose tasks aren't too sensitive.

- Barkl's morning routine begins with reading. He does this before even brushing, because postponing it to later never works out. By the time he is done bathing and eating, he is geared to go to work. When he returns home, he finds that the calm and serenity needed for him to settle down with a book just isn't there.

- Barkl considers TikTok to be one of the junk foods he enjoys. This is because, over time, his Twitter feed has been curated to provide information on tech and startup related news. On TikTok, however, he can just enjoy life hack videos and other forms of entertainment. Craigslist is another of Barkl's junk foods.

- Scott Fitsimones has a YouTube channel that he started in 2009. It presently has 390 subscriptions, about 7000 total views, and 14 videos. His last upload was from three years ago, and it bears the title "Pocket Collier Video Demo."

Tips for Emerging Businesses

1. The development of every startup should be done in phases. As a budding entrepreneur, it is important that you do not believe that your initial business model will be flawless. This is rarely ever the case for successful businesses. In fact, the very meaning of growth and development defies the idea of a perfect starting model. Some changes will occur, many of which will be caused by the feedback loop between your brand and its consumers.

    This is why there must be an open and easy channel of communication between you and your customers. You might modify or introduce new things, only to have customers complain and state their true needs. As such, be open and prepare for a phased growth. AirGarage, for instance, began with Google forms as a way to take in requests and connect drivers with available parking lots. As you might have predicted, this model was not efficient in managing the volume of requests that was coming in daily. So, they switched to an app designed by Fitsimones. Today, they have a more fine-tuned process of managing their orders.

2. Even for brands like AirGarage that began as a way to solve a personal problem, the business must eventually grow to take their customers' pain points into consideration. This is necessary if you want to broaden your customer base and stay ahead of the competition. Find out what the biggest complaints are in your industry, and scale your business by solving them.

   Founders of startups need to understand that as revolutionary and in-demand as their business might be, there is always the need to feel the market to know what more can be improved. They must seek new ways to make their customers' lives comfortable.

3. You've probably heard so much about mentorship from self-help gurus and successful entrepreneurs that you might be suspicious about it being just a useless buzzword at this point. The truth is that, especially for new founders, there is always so much more to know about business than can be read on the internet or in books.

Mentors are people who started their businesses, for the most part, clueless about what it would take to succeed. Through years of experience and by finding their own mentors, they unlearned disadvantageous behaviors and gained skills that not only helped them win, but stay on top too. Unless you are fine with wasting time by making mistakes that could easily be avoided, then you should reach out to mentors who are experienced and willing to share their wisdom with you.

Thankfully, finding and reaching out to mentors is much easier today than ever before in history. And this is all because of social media. Many of your favorite business people are on platforms like Instagram, Twitter, and LinkedIn. The only problem now would be getting replies from them. Remember that humility, patience, and politeness go a long way in getting someone to be your mentor. You can also increase your chances by sending emails and DMs to as many potential mentors as you can find. If you reach out to 100 business leaders and entrepreneurs, then at least two to 10% of them should reply.

Do not beat yourself up about not securing mentorship after trying your hardest. Although it helps to have a guide to help you navigate the world of business, it is not a necessity for success.

4. It is understandable that you would be nervous about trusting other people (especially strangers) with important aspects of your business. Also, many entrepreneurs are uncomfortable with the idea that they might be the least knowledgeable or qualified in certain key jobs that keep the business running smoothly. But if productivity and longevity are your goals for your brand, then you must do away with such feelings and be open to having other people take care of your baby—which might be how you view your startup.

You should hire as many competent people as is necessary to ensure company growth. Make sure that 90% of your employees are seasoned workers in their area of expertise. The other 10% can be those who, although qualified, may need some training before they are handed any real responsibilities.

And remember to delegate too. Make sure that you are not constantly looking over the shoulders of your team members and scrutinizing each step they take. Indeed, everyone loves a leader whose actions can be an example to their subordinates. But micromanaging will only negatively affect morale and create an atmosphere of distrust within the company.

Hire people who can make your job, as the leader, much easier. Then, do the scary but ultimately right thing and let go.

Chapter 11:

Advice for New

Entrepreneurs

In business, different roads can lead to success. This means that you needn't take *every* piece of advice you are given as an entrepreneur. See how the pointers fit into your peculiar situation and how valid they are before applying them. This includes the tips in this chapter.

Even though they can improve your chances of establishing a flourishing business, you should only take those ones that are best suited for your startup.

1. Know thyself. This is timeless wisdom, especially for first time entrepreneurs. Before you spend your time and resources researching the market, you must look inwards to determine if you have the right qualities that are needed to lead a startup to success.

   In a sense, you are to be the first interviewee for your company. If you are introverted and cannot bring yourself to cold call, cold email, or physically approach prospective investors, then you might want to consider bringing in a partner. Imagine the worst-case scenario and ask yourself if you are resilient, motivated, and resourceful enough to go the distance.

2. It is often better to develop your business idea in a field that you are familiar with. The founders of KiwiCo and Funnel are good examples of this. They both had the technological expertise that was needed to keep up with the industries they had chosen. While you might come upon a good idea that is mostly outside your realm of knowledge and experience, you stand a better chance at success if you comprehend your field of business.

   Be careful that you do not start your company solely on the fact that a particular industry is 'hot' at the moment.

3. If you already have an idea and are excited about it, this still isn't the time for you to launch. Before then, you should ascertain the feasibility of the business.
   - What will be required to make the business successful?
   - How long will it take for you to be profitable?

- Do people need your solution, and how much is the demand?
- What is the population size of your potential customer base?

It is important that you ask these questions and find honest answers to them.

4. Now, it's time to write a business plan. Feel free to search online for templates on convincing business plans. After all, you might need to present them to investors.

   Regardless of what you find online, make sure it includes the mission statement of your brand, a comprehensive description of your target market, product offerings, cost of operation, financial projections, executive summary, and company summary.

   Your business plan should be easy to understand and honest. Your financial projections must be based in facts and not on your hopes or as a way to deceive your partners and investors. If you do it right, even when you are questioned about your numbers, you can easily provide sources and confidently explain why your startup will be a winner.

5. You need to draw up a marketing plan. To do this, you must factor in how much money you currently have to work with, and how best they

can be allocated. You need money for basically every step of the development of your startup. You must spend on the production, distribution, and, if required, improvement of your product offerings.

You will also have to spend money to get the word about your brand out there. If budgeting and accounting are not among your strengths, then this might be the time to hire your first employee(s).

For instance, depending on your relationship with the accountant, your lean financial resources, and how much this worker believes in and can contribute to your business, it might be prudent to bring them on as a partner. If they agree to a percentage of the business, you can save the money that would have been spent on their salary.

6. Don't forget to make sure that your business name stays as yours. This means that you must register it with the appropriate office in your country.

Although it doesn't seem like this should require any urgency, business names are often personal and a part of why an entrepreneur might be motivated. This means that if you lose the trademark to another business, you may not have the same passion and energy as you did.

Also, none of this is complete until you have secured your domain name. Your company needs a website, and while it isn't compulsory, it should be the same as your brand name. You also want to use your brand name for your company's social media accounts. It might be best that you set up your social media before officially registering the business or paying for a domain name. That way, to the best of your abilities, you can make sure that your name is the same on all platforms.

7. It's not often the case that entrepreneurs start their companies from a place of personal financial strength. Most of the time, this resource is limited and will not suffice to help the business grow. As such, you might need seed funding to make sure that your company continues to exist.

   If your startup is yet to prove itself in the market, in regards to demand and sales, then you will have to communicate your passion to potential investors. This often requires some storytelling. Detail the origins of your idea and explain its benefits to consumers. Remember your data-driven and honest business plan? Present it to the investors. Talk about your business model and how much of your time, energy, and financial resources have gone into making the idea work. Next, let them know how they can help you.

But the most important thing to the majority of investors is knowing what they stand to gain by supporting your vision. As such, it is best to wrap up your discussion on this note. It is also beneficial to seek out investors that share your passion and will be easy to work with.

In many cases, an investor is someone who also started their business from nothing and nurtured its growth. As such, they might have suggestions and advice for you regarding your company. While you don't necessarily have to apply what they tell you to do, it is important that you listen. And make sure you are genuine about it too. Oftentimes, we are unable to see the ways in which our decisions are flawed, and might need a different perspective. This means that listening to your investors can be a win-win for you and them. That is, you get constructive criticism and suggestions that you are, depending on the nature of your agreement, not compelled to apply. Also, your investors can feel heard and appreciate the fact that you consider them to be a vital part of your business.

8. Starting any business can be especially demanding in a number of ways. It is both financially and emotionally tasking. As such,

your founders and family members should be on board for emotional support. Let them know that you may not be available for functions that, in the past, you were always present for. Your spouse or romantic partner should also be prepared for how frequently tired you might be.

They should be able to cheer you up and encourage you when the proverbial chips are down. It is also a plus if your loved ones can help you financially. Just be sure that you do not demand anything from them.

You may have heard it said that no one is an island. This adage encourages people to keep their loved ones close, because life is more difficult when you have to deal with it on your own. Arguably, entrepreneurs need people in their corner more than anyone else. If you have chosen to start your one business, then make sure to constantly update your friends and family members with details. They might notice a few things that you missed and bring it to your notice.

But more than all these is how much strength can be gotten from the genuine care, affection, and support of your loved ones.

9. Spend more time and resources taking care of and retaining existing customers than trying to

attract new ones. You should keep in mind that no one can sell your business better than a satisfied and loyal customer. So, carry out surveys to find out how you can serve your old customers better, and offer new products and services that show how well you listened.

10. Human beings are imperfect. As much as we strive for perfection in our various passions, it is often certain imperfections that we notice about other people that makes us trust and love them. We find it relatable. This accounts for why winning startups do not try to hide their failures and imperfections. Instead, while constantly trying to improve and stay ahead of their competition, they blog and make social media posts about their successes and struggles.

    You should do the same thing. Make jokes and create heartfelt stories about your business struggles. Allow your customers to root for and celebrate with you.

11. For any startup to thrive, its founders must work in harmony and be focused. Disagreements are sure to arise when different people are trying to decide on the direction that a business must move in. But if this is not resolved quickly, it could mean the downfall of your company.

If it happens that you and your business partner are constantly on opposing ends in the decision-making process, it might be time to dissolve the partnership.

12. This doesn't always happen but, at some point, you might have to give up a percentage of your business. If you need investors to come in, they will very likely want a stake in the company. If external investments are the only solution to the growth of your startup, then you shouldn't worry about giving up some control. Accept that other people must now be included in the decision-making process, and move on.

13. For your social media posts, blogs, and newsletters, you should hire a professional copywriter. These individuals are able to improve brand awareness and brand image by creating eye-grabbing content.

14. Even though you should try to stay ahead of the competition, recognize that having them is not a bad thing. In fact, competition is the best way to prove that there is a ready market for your idea. As such, don't be angry that they exist. And do not express your distaste of the competition to your investors or customers.

15. Companies are of different kinds. Yours might be a nonprofit, a limited liability, or a cooperative. This must be discussed with a

lawyer. There are many other legal aspects of your business that, if ignored, may lead to future problems and crush your startup. For instance, it is not enough to settle for a verbal agreement with your business partner or investor. And drawing up a contract is not as straightforward as you might imagine.

Let an experienced and trusted corporate lawyer advice you on the correct legal steps to take.

16. Tax obligations are different for self-employed individuals, employees, small businesses, non-profits, and so on. Keeping track of all that is necessary when filing taxes can be arduous for someone who hasn't been trained in this field. But more than the stress is the fact that you can make, literally, costly errors. This is why entrepreneurs are often advised to pay CPAs to help them with their taxes. These professionals can, indeed, be somewhat expensive, so you might want to take the state of your finances into consideration.

If you can afford to hire one, you will find that they are more than worth their fees in relation to the money that they will save your company.

17. Still on the necessary legalities, you should find out what licenses are compulsory for your

business to operate in the area that it's in. Imagine setting up shop and being optimistic, only to have it closed down after a short while. Even worse, getting penalized to some degree by the government. This could very well mean that all of your hard work and the efforts of your team have all been for nothing.

To avoid such an unfortunate occurrence, you should apply and get the needed licenses and permits.

18. No one starts a business hoping to get robbed, or that valuable items would be destroyed due to some unforeseen circumstance. Everyone hopes for the best. But as the saying goes, you should also expect the worst.

The possibility exists that certain calamitous events could happen. What you want to do is prepare for them and prevent financial setbacks. This is why insurances are a must for business owners. They can come in handy if there's a workplace injury, theft, or property damage.

Of course, the kind of insurance that is available to you depends on the kind of business you operate. So, you should go to trusted insurance companies who will guide you through the process.

19. Where will you be setting up shop? Where will your office be located? Where will you be storing inventory? Once you have learned all that is necessary about your business, attended to the legal aspects, and set things in motion, then it might be time to find a location for your business.

It should be in an area that is in close proximity to both your suppliers and customers. This way, you have created an opportunity for your business to grow quickly. There are instances where you just can't find the right location yet, or do not have enough funds to rent a space. Don't stress over this. Thanks to the internet, you can figure out a way for your business to be managed online, at least until you are able to have a physical office and store.

20. It's possible to believe that your ideas are so original that you want certain aspects of your business model to be patented. This issue with this is that enforcing a patent can be quite expensive. In the United States, for instance, it costs anywhere between $2500 and $4000 to register a patent. And to make sure it's done right, you might have to hire the services of a lawyer. This means additional costs that will most likely adversely affect your infant business.

If your startup is not profitable enough to afford a patent, and you are unable to get it done out of pocket, then consider waiting until this decision will not lead to the failure of your business.

21. One thing every founder in this book has in common is that, at some point, their founders had to either pivot or modify their original idea to serve a bigger need. You should be open to the fact that, as helpful as your idea is right now and despite the demand that exists for it, you might have to change some aspects of your brand to serve your customers better.

    The way in which you carry out any change to your brand and products will determine the longevity and success of your business. It should be managed in such a way that your existing customers remain interested and potential clients are attracted to your business.

22. As much as sharing your business ideas with loved ones can be helpful, you need to be careful about who you consider a trustworthy friend or family member. You want to avoid sabotage or getting drowned in negative opinions.

    Constructive criticism is quite different from being a naysayer. If a certain individual can only ever tell you why your ideas are sure to fail, then it might be best to stop divulging secrets about your business to them.

23. Regardless of how you feel about your idea, you cannot impose it on the market. Instead, consumers dictate which brands win or lose. Your reaction to how the market feels about your product offerings could make all the difference in your business. If you get angry at customers and investors who do not like your idea, then that might just be the end of your startup.

The better approach is to calmly ask what they do not like about your idea, and their opinions on how it can be improved. It could, in fact, be that the problem is not with the product itself. The timing or branding could just be wrong. See the market's rejection as a way to fine-tune your company until it is just what consumers need.

Of course, there's also the chance that you've had a bad idea and might need to move on from it.

24. Don't waste time waiting for the perfect moment to enter the market. Start delivering now. There is nothing more important to a brand than the community that forms around it.

And the earlier you start promoting your brand, the faster you can grow a community that supports and is loyal to you.

25. Word of mouth is the best marketing strategy for any business. You want to have people talking about your business and converting new customers, even when you're not running an ad. The only way to enjoy the benefits of word of mouth is to focus on the quality of your products, delivery, and customer service. Ensure that your products are beautifully packaged and work as promised. Also, get the products to your customers on time, and hire competent customer service agents who will represent your brand well.

26. You've got to mingle. Even if you're an introvert who is terrified of social interactions, networking is the best way to learn new information about your industry, find out ways to improve as an entrepreneur, and make friends with potential investors. In some cases, it is also helpful to organize small get-togethers with a few of your most loyal customers.

Chapter 12:

33 Facts About Startups

1. If you are currently working for someone, regardless of how long you've spent in your nine to five, don't give up hope about establishing your own company someday. 70% of entrepreneurs get their business idea while working for someone else.

2. Most founders do not spend an appropriate amount of time considering the equity split with their business partners and investors. 80% of them make this crucial decision in less than an hour. One reason for this is that new entrepreneurs are never too convinced that they will become profitable.

3. 94% of the founders of the most successful businesses are men. There are any number of reasons that anyone can come up with to explain this statistic, but the most common one is that most women prefer the security of a stable income, and might be unwilling to risk the uncertainty of entrepreneurship.

4. Only 75% of startups make it past the first year. Whether this is comforting or scary, it is the next few years that are even more crucial. This is because half of all new businesses fail in five years.

5. The more time that passes, the greater the chance that your business will fail. In fact, there is a 60% chance that you will close up shop on or before the 10th year of running your business.

6. The number one reason why many businesses never succeed is also quite obvious: they offer a product or service that consumers don't want. Even the best branding experts with a seemingly inexhaustible marketing budget are likely to fail when consumers do not like its offerings.

7. If you avoid or gain knowledge on the three heralds of business failure, then you can increase your chances of becoming profitable and survive the four-year startup statistic. They include the lack of experience, fraud, and incompetence. Experience includes both the entrepreneurial and managerial aspects—both of which can be aided by reading books, listening to interviews by other business leaders, and getting a mentor.

8. Unicorn companies are startups that are worth at least a billion dollars or more. They are aptly named for how rare they are. However, the number of unicorns have been growing rapidly in recent years. In 2018, there were 174 startups. Today, there are 546 startups that are valued at a billion dollars or more.

9. If you are wondering which technological industries are the most populated, then consider these:
   a. 7.1% of startups are in fintech
   b. 6.8% of startups are in life sciences and health-care
   c. 5% of startups are in artificial intelligence
   d. 4.7% of startups are in gaming
   e. 3.3% of startups are in adtech
   f. 2.8% of startups are in edtech
   g. 2.1% of startups are in cleantech
   h. 1.5% of startups are in blockchain
   i. 1.3% of startups are in robotics
   j. 0.7% of startups are in cybersecurity
   k. 0.6% of startups are in agtech

10. The location of your company, as it concerns the level of your profitability, might be a factor. 50% of all unicorn companies are located in the United States. China comes in second, with 25% of unicorns located in their country. The

United Kingdom and India regularly switch between third and fourth place, with about 5% of unicorn companies.

11. Aside from misreading what the market wants or needs, running low on cash is the second biggest reason why startups fail. 29% of failed businesses are attributed to running out of funds.

12. The individuals who make up your founding team must be motivated and competent. Starting with a weak team is the third biggest reason why many businesses shut down. 23% of the time, an incompetent and dispassionate team is why startups fail.

13. Regardless of the industry you work in, you will probably have stiff and well-established competition. To increase your chances of success, you should do some research on the competition. There's an 18% chance that your business might fail because of superior competition.

14. Many would-be entrepreneurs often point to success stories of Bill Gates, Elon Musk, and Mark Zuckerberg as reasons why they should drop out of school. But you might be surprised to know that 95% of all founders of startups have at least a bachelor's degree.

15. Don't worry about not having the resources to rent an office space. You are not alone. 69% of startups began in the homes of the founders. But there might be some benefit to working from home, as more than 50% of entrepreneurs continue to work from home, even after their business starts yielding profits.

16. Age might also increase one's likelihood of being a successful entrepreneur. Indeed, 60-year-old entrepreneurs are three times more likely to grow a profitable startup than their 30-year-old contemporaries. So, if you think that you're too old to start your own business, you are probably wrong.

17. You would think that people who have had some success with a previous business are sure to win with a new business. In reality, they've only got a 30% chance of succeeding with a new venture.

18. Previously successful founders fare better than those who have failed at other businesses. There is a 20% chance that their new business will go the distance and be profitable.

19. Statistically, it *is* better to have tried and failed than shy from trying entirely. If you are a first-time entrepreneur, then there's an 18% chance that your startup will flourish.

20. The customer is king. However, 14% of startups refuse to acknowledge this fact, and they go out of business.

21. If you are about to meet with investors, then you should know that one in four businesses will not be able to secure funding. While the likelihood is that you will get investors to fund your startup, you should make sure that you have prepared well to meet with them.

22. Three of the most expensive industries to join are medical offices, restaurants, and manufacturing companies. If you have founded a startup in any of these fields, then be prepared to spend as much as $100,000 to start your business.

23. If you are months into your business and are yet to hire workers, this is not peculiar. On average, founders take up to six months before employing people. So, don't rush it. But you should bring people in when working alone starts to affect the growth of your company.

24. How many employees would you say it takes to increase the chances of a startup's failure? The range is between 11 and 50 workers. If you have less than 11 or more than 50 workers, then this statistic is in your favor.

25. Two founders are better than one. This means that you should consider getting a business

partner, since having one raises the odds of the success of your startup by 30%. It also improves the rate of customer growth by three.

26. If you believe that you will someday have to sell your company, then you're among the 57% of founders who also envision the same thing. In fact, only 16% of startup business owners wanted to remain privately owned. 18% of startups will be publicly listed, and there are 9% of founders who have no long-term ambitions for their companies.

27. Be sure that you are not starting a company and leaving your old job because you hate working long hours. This is because 89% of small business owners work even on weekends. In fact, 20% of founders work up to 59 hours a week, and another 30% work up to 49 hours a week. So, if you choose entrepreneurship and desire success, be ready to work overtime.

28. If you're a founder and you believe that artificial intelligence is the future of technology, then you are among the 60% of entrepreneurs who share the same vision. They project that AI, as it affects cleantech, will see more investors banking on the industry.

29. In 2016, there were 4.8 million small businesses in America alone. In 2020, this number grew to 31.7 million. It is entirely within the realm of

possibility that, in about 25 to 30 years, every American would have a startup.

30. The time taken to establish a startup varies according to the country. In America, you can be up and running in five days, but it takes more than 100 days for founders to start their businesses in Brazil.

31. From 1997 to 2005, the number of businesses owned by female entrepreneurs grew by 74%. African American women, in particular, are the fastest group of founders. The number of businesses owned by this group has increased by more than 322% since 1997.

32. For a while, Uber was the most valuable startup in the world with a valuation of $72 billion. But they were overtaken by ByteDance in 2018. This company operates TikTok, and it was valued at $78 billion in 2018. It retains the number one spot today with a valuation of $140 billion.

33. A 2009 report showed that more than 50% of Fortune 500 companies that were listed that year were founded during a bear market 0r recession. This proves that, while the economy can affect startups, the perseverance and resourcefulness of business owners are the biggest determining factor for success.

Conclusion

Few things can beat the high of having what you believe is a solid idea, defeating the hurdles that would prevent your business from taking off, and finally actualizing your dream.

While it is nearly impossible that most of us will be billionaires, the odds are not nearly as high when it concerns building a stable and profitable business. It is achievable.

But as you may have learned from the entrepreneurs discussed in the book, success is dependent on action. The choices you make and the things you refrain from doing will determine how far you will go with your winning idea.

Let the success stories in this book and the lessons packed in them give you the wings to fly and the courage to jump.

References

Alan. (2020, April 6). *Funnel.io quadruples revenue to $10 million, raises $47 million, at a $200 million valuation.* Latka. https://blog.getlatka.com/funnel-io-revenue-fundraise-customers/

Cetera, M. (2016, June 13). Survey: surprisingly few millennials carry credit cards. Bankrate. https://www.google.com/amp/s/www.bankrate.com/finance/consumer-index/money-pulse-0616.aspx/amp/

Chicks we love: an interview with Sarah Oh Lin of KiwiCo & her advice for female entrepreneurs. ChipChick. https://www.chipchick.com/2019/06/chicks-we-love-an-interview-with-sandra-oh-lin-of-kiwico-her-advice-for-female-entrepreneurs.html

Cremades, A. (n.d.) *Fredrik Skantze on being forced to close down his first business and now raising $65M to prepare marketing data for better reporting.* Alejandro Cremades. https://alejandrocremades.com/fredrik-skantze/#:~:text=Fredrik%20Skantze%20is%20CEO%20and,Degree%20in%20Engineering%20from%20MIT.

Davis, T. & Amber. (2017, December 1). *How does she do it: Eliza Blank of The Sill.* Forbes. https://www.forbes.com/sites/contextandco/2017/12/01/how-does-she-do-it-eliza-blank-of-the-sill/?sh=20c477a34889

Drori, D. (2020, November 3). *How The Sill's founder turned $32,000 into a multimillion-dollar plant business.* The Helm. https://thehelm.co/the-sill-eliza-blank-interview/

Eliza Blank. (2017, March). Bird. https://www.wearebird.co/eliza-blank

Family ties: introducing Eliza Blank. (n.d.). Blank Studio. https://www.blankstudionyc.com/community-highlights/eliza-blank-interview

Kauflin, J. (2018, July 3). How a 28-year-old turned layaway for millennials into a billion-dollar business. Forbes. https://www.google.com/amp/s/www.forbes.com/sites/jeffkauflin/2018/07/03/how-a-28-year-old-turned-layaway-for-millennials-into-a-2-billion-business/amp/

Kelly, S. (2021). 31 public companies founded by women. Thestoryexchange. https://www.google.com/amp/s/thestoryexchange.org/31-public-companies-founded-women/amp/

Lagorio-Chafkin, C. (2019, April 18). *Mountain View mom asks: is this little idea a viable business? She turned it into a $100 million one.* Inc. https://www.inc.com/christine-lagorio-chafkin/kiwico-is-the-subscription-box-company-to-beat.html

Party. (2020, June 9). *6 easy steps to make money selling house plants.* Medium. https://enhorning-p.medium.com/6-easy-steps-to-make-money-selling-house-plants-aad013c9a88f

Rider, J. (2018, July 8). *Your vc needs a billion dollar exit. You do not.* Crunchbase News. https://news.crunchbase.com/news/your-vc-needs-a-billion-dollar-exit-you-do-not/

Shethwala, M. (2019, October 30). *What are the odds of you becoming a millionaire.* Medium. https://medium.com/@miteshshethwala/what-are-the-odds-of-you-becoming-a-billionaire-f03cf48b4932

Stangler, D. (2009). *The economic future just happened.* Kauffman. https://www.kauffman.org/entrepreneurship/reports/the-economic-future-just-happened/

Villegas, S. (2020, May 15). *"It almost needs to be both your work and hobby at the same time": interview with Funnel's CEO Fredrik Skantze.* EU-Startups. https://www.eu-startups.com/2020/05/it-almost-needs-to-be-both-your-work-and-hobby-at-the-same-time-interview-with-funnels-ceo-fredrik-skantze/

Why it matters. (n.d.). Power To Decide. https://powertodecide.org/what-we-do/information/why-it-matters

Woo, M. (2018, August 13). I'm Sarah Oh Lin, founder of KiwiCo, and this is how I parent. Lifehacker. https://offspring.lifehacker.com/im-sandra-oh-lin-founder-of-kiwico-and-this-is-how-i-1828299023

Zimmerman, E. (2018, April 1). Only 2% of women-owned businesses break the $1million mark - here's how to be one of them. Forbes. https://www.google.com/amp/s/www.forbes.com/sites/eilenezimmerman/2015/04/01/only-2-of-women-owned-businesses-break-the-1-million-mark-heres-how-to-be-one-of-them/amp/